The Manager's Coaching Toolkit

PEARSON
Prentice Hall
BUSINESS

Books that make you better

Books that make you better. That make you *be* better, *do* better, *feel* better. Whether you want to upgrade your personal skills or change your job, whether you want to improve your managerial style, become a more powerful communicator, or be stimulated and inspired as you work.

Prentice Hall Business is leading the field with a new breed of skills, careers and development books. Books that are a cut above the mainstream – in topic, content and delivery – with an edge and verve that will make you better, with less effort.

Books that are as sharp and smart as you are.

Prentice Hall Business.
We work harder – so you don't have to.

For more details on products, and to contact us, visit
www.pearsoned.co.uk

The Manager's Coaching Toolkit

Fast and simple solutions for busy managers

Dr David Allamby

Harlow, England • London • New York • Boston • San Francisco • Toronto
Sydney • Tokyo • Singapore • Hong Kong • Seoul • Taipei • New Delhi
Cape Town • Madrid • Mexico City • Amsterdam • Munich • Paris • Milan

PEARSON EDUCATION LIMITED

Edinburgh Gate
Harlow CM20 2JE
Tel: +44 (0) 1279 623623
Fax: +44 (0) 1279 431059
Website: www.pearsoned.co.uk

First published in Great Britain in 2006

ISBN-13: 978-0-273-70831-5
ISBN-10: 0-273-70831-7

British Library Cataloguing-in-Publication Data
A catalogue record for this book is available from the British Library

Library of Congress Cataloging-in-Publication Data
The coaching toolkit: Fast and simple solutions for busy managers / David Allamby.
    p. cm.
  Includes index.
  ISBN-13: 978-0-273-70831-5 (alk. paper)
  ISBN-10: 0-273-70831-7 (alk. paper)
  1. Employees--Coaching of.   2. Teams in the workplace--Management.   3. Employee
motivation.

  HF5549.5.C53C638 2006
  658.3'14--dc22

          2006050070

10 9 8 7 6 5 4 3 2 1
10 09 08 07 06

Typeset in 10.25pt Minion by 3
Printed and bound in Great Britain by Bell & Bain Ltd, Glasgow

The publisher's policy is to use paper manufactured from sustainable forests.

Contents

Toolkit icon summary   vii
Introduction   ix
Coaching toolkit roadmap – which tool to use and when   xvi

Chapter 1 How to hold a coaching conversation   1

*Structure every coaching discussion to cover the five key stages –
every time you* **COACH**   1

Chapter 2 Following up on a coaching session   15

*Helping others learn from experience and behave in new ways –
a tool worth its weight in* **GOLD!**   15

Chapter 3 Setting goals with a plan built in   29

The calm after this **STORM** *is because you know what you want and
where you're going*   29

Chapter 4 Giving feedback that works   45

*Make sure your feedback can be easily swallowed and digested – give
it in* **STAGES!**   45

Chapter 5 How to find the best solution to a problem   61

Use this tool when a problem **DROPS** *on to your desk!*   61

Chapter 6 Difficult decisions made easy   79

When there is a difficult decision, **OPERA** *can make things simple*   79

Chapter 7 Decision making now and in the future   99

*Too close to see where you are now? Unclear of your position? Stand
back and* **SWOT** *it!*   99

Chapter 8 Taking the pain out of performance appraisals   121

Reviewing performance can be daunting – break it down into six easy
STAGES!   121

Index   135

Toolkit icon summary

	How to use the tool	A detailed description of how to apply the tool in a real world situation
	Sample coaching conversation	Dialogues to demonstrate an experienced manager using the tool
	Where next?	How to follow up after having used a specific tool
	History of the tool	The background to the development of the tool from the author or others
	Related tools	Other tools often used together with the current one
	Further reading	Books to find out more on the tool, related models or key individuals
	Bright idea!	An action step or suggestion to improve learning or performance
	Learning point	A key learning point related to the adjacent main text
	Take action!	An action step you can take to start getting results straight away

Introduction

The problem

www.CoachingToolbook.com

Managers today are busier than they have ever been. It's a fact. As a manager, you have more responsibility, accountability and a heavier workload than ever before. You are also expected to develop your team members and help them to think for themselves. The need to develop coaching skills has never been more pressing and the time to do it never harder to find. It's not always possible to go on a coaching course or read detailed books on its theory and practice. Even if you do attend a course, it's not always easy to transfer that knowledge to the workplace.

The solution

This book is the answer for every manager who has wanted to learn or improve his or her coaching skills. It will simulate the experience of sitting in with a master manager coach who utilizes a range of tools and skills for a wide variety of common workplace situations. Even with no previous knowledge, you can start coaching within 15 minutes of opening this book. It provides you with a compendium of models that can be applied quickly and easily to many of the everyday challenges that any manager will face, from conducting performance reviews to problem solving and beyond. All you have to do is find the appropriate tool from the situational roadmap guide, read the chapter and you're ready to go.

How to use the book

Select the relevant situations from the roadmap guide found on page xvi, just after this Introduction, and choose the appropriate tool listed underneath.

If you want to get started straight away (and, of course, you do!), you can go right to that chapter. You will find it is pretty self-explanatory. Come back and read this Introduction afterwards, as it gives advice on how to ask questions – an essential coaching skill.

This book gives you a simple sequence of actions to take you to a solution for each situation, with each one presented as a memorable acronym. Each chapter is arranged in the same way, and presents the information as a progression from the tool itself to a fuller understanding of how it works. Icons highlight the various sections of each chapter – see the Toolkit icon summary on page vii.

After a short introduction, you will see a graphic of the stages that make up the tool. Then, there are a series of bullet points and a short section telling you when and how the tool can be used. After that comes the first sample conversation, which demonstrates how it can be applied. The individual stages of the tool are emphasized in bold, so you can easily follow the steps. The example is then analysed in a little more depth, so that you can see how it works.

The second example of a coaching conversation gives you another scenario, with more detailed annotations, indicating the kind of questions being used and giving a few useful tips, or very short explanations of what is happening in the conversation, if it is not immediately clear. Under the heading, 'Where next?', you will find a paragraph telling you what you can do next and which tools to use to increase the impact and effectiveness of your session together. There is a very brief history of the tool – how it has evolved – followed by a list of links to other related tools in the book. You will also find recommended further reading for that particular area, should you wish to dive in deeper.

The chapter ends with a summary of the key learning points.

Each of these template guides can be downloaded from the toolkit website, **www.CoachingToolbook.com**. You then have everything you need. All you have to do is start coaching!

How each chapter is laid out

The coaching tool	A coaching tool – divided into stages in order to guide a conversation

When to use this tool	Typical situations where you could use the tool
How to use the tool	A detailed description of how to apply the tool in a real world situation

Sample coaching conversation	The first dialogue shows an experienced manager coach using the tool.
Unpacking the conversation	Analysing the coaching conversation, to see how the manager applied the tool, and hints on best practice

Second coaching conversation	The second dialogue shows the tool used in a different situation. More detailed notes on specific techniques used by the manager
Where next?	How to follow up after having used a specific tool
History of the tool	The background to the development of the tool from the author or others
Related tools	Other tools often used together with the current one
Further reading	Books to find out more on the tool, its background or related models
Learning points summary	A review of key points

Coach's notes	Space to make your own learning notes

Getting the climate right

Coaching is not only about asking questions and hearing what the other person is saying. Before you use each of the tools in this book, you need to create a climate of *TRUST* between you and your coachee:

***T**est the temperature*	Be aware of the other person's reactions and feelings
***R**espect the individual*	Treat the other person as an adult whose beliefs, values, opinions and ways of doing things may be different from your own
***U**nderstand their point of view*	Put yourself in their shoes
***S**ay it!*	You have to say what you've heard to check understanding
***T**ailor your approach*	Match your language and style to the other person's approach

Questioning, listening and responding

The three core skills of a great coach are asking the right questions, truly listening to what is said and responding in such a way as to move the conversation purposefully forwards.

Learning Point

Knowing what kind of questions to ask is a key coaching skill. Add to that knowing how to listen and you will be a great coach!

Listening

The most important tool you have as a coach is your ability to listen, which is not the same as your ability to hear. Good, careful listening is about giving your full attention to the other person, gathering clues from what is being said and picking up on what is not being said. As a guide, if you talk for more than 20 to 30 per cent of the time and listen for less than 70 per cent, you're not coaching!

Responding

The table below gives you a summary of the types of questions and responses that will be useful to you as a coach, with a brief description, when to use it and an example of each type.

QUESTIONS	What it is	When to use it	Example
Closed questions	Questions that elicit a 'yes' or 'no', or a two or three word answer	■ To control and shape the conversation ■ To check your understanding ■ To clarify a point ■ To close a topic ■ To change topic ■ To get the conversation back on track	**Coach:** You said you had a choice – either you leave tomorrow or next week. Is that right? *or* **Coach:** Who's best qualified for that position – Brad or Yoko?
Simple open questions	Questions that require a longer answer	To encourage the coachee to talk or give more information	Start with the words 'what', 'why', 'how' – for example: ■ What were the reasons behind your choice? ■ How will you achieve that? ■ Why did you select Michael?
Probing questions	A more complex kind of open question – often phrased as statements	When you want to find out more or delve deeper	■ Tell me more about... ■ Let's talk about... ■ I'm wondering whether...

QUESTIONS	What it is	When to use it	Example
Hypothesizing questions	A question that poses an alternative, challenges a statement or puts forward a suggestion	When you want to challenge, make a suggestion or get the coachee thinking in a different way	■ What if. . .? ■ What would happen if. . .? ■ How would it be if. . .? ■ Suppose. . .?
Clarifying questions	A question that requires the coachee to explain	When you want to clarify a point – or challenge a point	■ How would you explain. . .? ■ Are you saying that. . .?
RESPONSES	What it is	When to use it	Example
Paraphrasing	Saying what the other person has said in a different way	To show that you have listened, and to check understanding	**Coachee:** Reading takes up so much time **Coach:** You've been reading a lot recently *or* **Coachee:** I'm getting to the end of my tether **Coach:** You've had enough
Reflecting content	Repeating all or part of what the coachee has said	To show that you have heard what was said, and to encourage the coachee to continue	**Coachee:** I've finally completed that report **Coach:** OK, completed your report. . .

RESPONSES	What it is	When to use it	Example
Reflecting feelings	Acknowledging the coachee's state of mind in words	To show you are aware of how they are feeling	**Coachee:** My boss really let me down badly this time **Coach:** I can see that you are angry
Summarizing	Repeats and abbreviates the points the coachee has made	■ To check you've understood ■ To bring the discussion back to the point ■ To consolidate a number of points	**Coach:** You've identified three options. One – you could leave; two – you could stay and tough it out; and three – you could stay and keep your head down

Coaching toolkit roadmap – which tool to use and when

Use the COACH tool for most coaching conversations. This powerful yet flexible structure provides the questions the coachee needs to hear to discover solutions for themselves

Drill down to clarify each objective - where is the destination and what resources are needed to get there - plus how will the coachee measure their progress

Coaching conversation
COACH Ch. 1

Setting specific objectives
STORM Ch. 3

1 **2**

How do I complete a coaching cycle?

4 **3**

Give clear specific feedback
STAGES Ch. 4

Follow up on a coaching conversation
GOLD Ch. 2

Deepen learning with a structured feedback conversation where you discover the coachee's self-assessment, plus provide your own views on performance or results for each objective

Follow up on coaching conversations to enhance and accelerate learning. The GOLD tool quickly shows whether objectives were met and, crucially, how future behaviour needs to change

How to hold a coaching conversation

Structure every coaching discussion to cover the five key stages – every time you COACH

C	**Clarify** the topic
O	**Outcome** desired
A	**Actually** happening
C	**Create** options
H	**Hard copy** action plan

Visit:
www.CoachingToolbook.com

Coaching happens in conversations. It is a purposeful dis-cussion with a set number of standard parts. The COACH model contains all the elements you need to get effective results in a tremendously wide range of situations. This tool is lean and powerful – results without the waffle.

When to use this tool

⇒   Any time you need to coach.

⇒   When someone comes to you for help.

⇒   When you want someone to think through a problem for themselves, rather than being given the answer.

How to use the tool

Your job as a coach is to structure the conversation using the five stages of the COACH model to ensure that learners (who we also will call 'coachees') think through the problem or issue for themselves, clarify their understanding and create their own solutions. Each stage of the COACH sequence is essential to the process.

As you read through the following example conversation, notice how the coach uses a series of questions to encourage the coachee to gen-erate his or her own answers and so move from uncertainty to an effective solution.

We can summarize coaching quite simply: finding a way from A to B and learning from the process. As a coach, you will help to clarify where the starting point (A) is and help to determine where the destination

(B) lies. All that remains is to brainstorm all the possible routes from A to B, with their respective pros and cons, and to choose the best one. That's it! The structure of the questions, 'Where do I want to go?' 'Where am I now?' 'How best will I get to where I want to be?' and 'What have I learned about getting from A to B?' allows that person to discover, for themselves, the best route for any future journeys.

> Personally, I never like being taught, although I am always willing to learn.
>
> *Winston Churchill (1874–1965), statesman and prime minister*

Sample coaching conversation

In this example, the coachee is having difficulty chairing meetings of his project planning team and seeks help from his manager. Observe the series of guided questions used so that the coachee creates a clear action plan for himself.

Learning Point

'As the wise man said when the young man asked how he could get to Carnegie Hall – Practise, Practise, Practise!'

Coachee: You know I chair the project planning team for the integration of TechScan Corp. into our R&D division. We have met three times and I am having real trouble chairing the meetings. I need some help to get things back on track.

Manager: Of course, and I've got about 20 minutes if that's OK for you. Let's begin with **clarifying the topic**. What is it specifically that you would like help with?

Coachee: Well, the meetings so far have been pretty chaotic. They run on and on and we aren't making much progress. So I need help with how to run an effective meeting.

Manager: OK, the topic is clear so now clarify the **ideal outcome**. I want you to describe to me what it would look like. In practical terms, what would occur at a highly effective meeting?

Coachee: First, a one-hour meeting would last for one hour.

Manager: It would run to time. What else?

Coachee: We would set an agenda and stick to it, not go running off at a tangent like we have been doing.

Manager: Following an agenda and timing. Is there anything else that would happen at this perfect meeting?

Coachee: Yes, we would know clearly what actions will be taken afterwards.

Manager: OK, running to time, following the agenda and clarifying action steps. Tell me now what's **actually been happening** so far.

Coachee: We overrun, often by an hour or more, and still don't come out with anything solid. Afterwards I feel we haven't achieved what was necessary. I guess it's really down to my inexperience with being the chair. This is the first time I've had to do this.

Manager: Tell me more about how you set your agenda.

Coachee: Well, I say, 'We need to cover X, Y and Z,' and basically off we go!

Manager: OK, I have a clear picture now. Next, I want you to **create some options**, ideas about what you could do differently.

Coachee: Now that I have described it, some seem quite obvious! I could spend the first five minutes confirming the agenda. I could ask each member what he or she thinks we need to cover.

Manager: What else?

Coachee: Also allocating time blocks to each item. That way I know how the hour is divided up and when we need to speed things up to get on to the next item. I need to make sure any action steps are clarified, so we all know who's doing what.

Manager: How could you do that?

Coachee: I could put my watch on the table so I can keep track of time easily. And I must record any action points so that I can summarize at the end.

Manager: OK, you've produced some simple and clear steps ready for the next meeting. I want you to get this down on **hard copy as an action plan**. What action items are you going to commit to? Write them down as you tell me.

Take Action!

Write down how you can use this tool today – just one sentence is enough!

Coachee: Right. Number one, first five minutes to set the agenda, and two, agree on time allocation. Three, make sure I can see the time to track our progress. Four, clarify each action item and who will be doing it. I'll try this and see how it goes.

Unpacking the conversation

Learning Point

Remember: a good outcome can be measured or observed.

Now, read on for an analysis of the conversation in more depth.

In this example, the topic was quickly determined to be 'chairing an effective meeting', and so both people were clear what the subject of the session was to be. Next, the coach wanted the coachee to define the ideal destination (B) in simple measurable terms, i.e. the outcome:

Manager: OK, the topic is clear so now clarify the **ideal outcome**. I want you to describe to me what it would look like. In practical terms, what would occur at a highly effective meeting?

The coach used a very useful phrase, asking 'what it [the outcome] would look like', to help the coachee define the best possible result. The coach's job in this part of the COACH tool is to push for a measurable or observable outcome – something that could be seen by the coachee or an observer. Often a number could define it – e.g. finishing work at 6pm or producing five reports per week. If the goal is less tangible, e.g. 'chairing a meeting effectively' as in the sample conversation, it needs to be defined in terms of the behaviours that would be different, such as 'agree on the time allocation'.

Note how the coach uses open questions to bring out the widest range of information from the coachee – for example, 'In practical terms, what would occur at a highly effective meeting?' and 'What else?' Once you know where the coachee needs to get to, next comes the starting point (A). This is a description of what is actually happening right now. Again, ask open questions to elicit as much information as you need to see a full picture. The coachee may discover a solution simply through clearly describing what has been tried unsuccessfully. Stepping outside the situation and looking inwards with the coach may be enough to show the way forward.

Most likely, however, is that you would ask the coachee to create various options to facilitate the move from A to B. You would then write down each suggestion to make a list:

Manager: OK, I have a clear picture now. Next, I want you to **create some options**, ideas about what you could do differently.

Coachee: [Coachee produces one or two options]

Manager: What else?

The first one or two suggestions you record will be things the coachee has already thought of and possibly tried unsuccessfully. As a coach, you need to dig to get the ideas that are just below the surface. With gentle probing such as 'What else?' you will allow the coachee to create new ideas of their own. You may also offer your own ideas, but only after the coachee has run out or drawn a blank. You will frequently discover that the coachee already has the answers they need, but just needs some encouragement to bring them out.

Learning Point

If you don't write an action plan down, you have just been talking!

The final and critical stage of the COACH process is to help the coachee to select the best action step(s) and get them down on paper, i.e. make a hard copy action plan. If the action items are not written down for the coachee to go away and implement, you may have been having a good conversation, but it wasn't coaching! Notice how our coach phrased it:

Manager: OK, you've produced some simple and clear steps ready for the next meeting. I want you to get this down on **hard copy as an action plan**. What action items are you going to commit to? Write them down as you tell me.

The first step to accountability is to get the coachee to select the best options from those just created and write them down as an action plan. As coach, you will also make a copy. The next time you meet you can refer to your list and see what was done and how well it went.

The action plan should be specific: What will be done? When will it happen? Who else will be involved? What resources will be needed? Creating this level of detail will assist the coachee in carrying out each action step (see the STORM goals in Chapter 3).

Note: As with each of the various coaching tools in this book, you don't need to have particular expertise or special knowledge relating to the topic. The tools are designed so that you can guide the coachee through a sequence of questions, so that they can discover the answers for themselves.

Second coaching conversation

The following example from the first coaching conversation, where the coachee said that he would try. The brackets contain notes about techniques the coach used and the individual stages of the COACH tool:

Manager: You've said that you'll try to follow the action points we've generated. You don't sound very confident! **(Notices and acknowledges the temperature)** Is there anything else that you want to clarify? **(Probing question)**

Coachee: Well, yes. I'm still not sure how I'm going to get these people to move on to a different agenda item when the allocated time is up.

Manager: OK. Let's look at how you can move on to the next item on an agenda. **(Clarify the topic)**

What would a smooth change look like if this problem didn't exist? **(Outcome desired. Miracle question)**

Coachee: We'd wrap up the topic within the allotted time, with an agreed action plan. Then I'd announce the next subject and we'd move on.

Manager: Sounds good. So what actually happens now? **(Actually happening)**

Coachee: Either someone raises another issue and people discuss that while the others get frustrated, or we go round in circles and it drags on.

Manager: I think there are two separate issues here. **(Clarifies the topic further by paraphrasing)** First, how to keep to time, and second, how to keep the discussions on track. We don't have time in this session to explore both. Which one do you want to look at now?

Coachee: Timekeeping is probably the most important.

Manager: Can you think of anything you could do, as chair? **(Create options)**

Coachee: This is where I get stuck – I don't know where to start.

Manager: Have you ever been in a well-run meeting? **(Changes tack – prompts the coachee to use their experience of a similar situation)**

Coachee: Yes, actually, I have. Nick is a very good chairperson.

Manager: What does he do to keep it to time? **(Specific open question)**

Coachee: He always has an agenda – oh, and he warns everyone that we're running out of time for the subject a few minutes before. I could do that – then wrap it up.

Manager: Giving a timely warning is a great action step. **(Confirms and encourages)** Now, how could you wrap it up and move on?

Coachee: (The coach gives him time to think) I could facilitate the end in stages – say that there are five minutes to go, to give time to finish off, then say that we must move on, summarize the discussion and write down the actions there and then.

> **Learning Point**
>
> A '**miracle question**' asks the coachee to imagine the scenario as if the problem did not exist – a good way of getting coachees to focus on the outcome, not the problem.
>
> The coachee has then to describe the observable differences and behaviours.

Learning Point

Use silence to give coachees time to think, when appropriate.

Learning Point

Don't lose sight of issues you didn't have time to explore. Agree a time to continue.

Manager: Right, you've come up with a few good ideas. Let's summarize the action points and write them down like we did before. **(Hard copy action plan)**

Coachee: OK. **(Talks through the actions and writes them down, as before)**

Manager: Let's arrange a time to talk through options for keeping the discussions on track.

At the end of the first sample conversation, the coach noticed the temperature of the session and picked up on the lukewarm response, 'I'll try this and see how it goes.' She acknowledges this and probes to find out where the uncertainty lies. She then uses the COACH model again – it can be used several times in one conversation if there is more than one issue to be addressed.

The coach used a solution-focused coaching approach. Sometimes it is possible simply to acknowledge what is actually happening right now, without analysing it. Instead, the focus is on the desired result. The coach has asked about the ideal outcome by getting the coachee to imagine how things would be if the problem miraculously no longer existed (known as the 'miracle question'). The focus is away from the problems and on possible solutions.

Where next?

Having created a hard copy action plan and put it into effect, the coachee will typically experience a varying degree of success. Often, just making some small adjustment as a result of the coaching after having been stuck with a problem is enough to facilitate change. Creating a comprehensive 12-step programme is not necessary. A more helpful approach is to generate one or two simple steps that the coachee can put into practice, and then he or she can come back for a follow-up session.

Once you have generated some action steps together, the most useful tool for follow up and review is the GOLD model in Chapter 2 (provided you do not have any issues outstanding, as in our second conversation). This allows you to maximize learning by utilizing the way that adults normally learn – from experience. Guiding the conversations with the GOLD sequence will enhance learning for this and subsequent actions. Set a date/time to talk together again after your COACH session(s). Read the next chapter and you are ready to follow up.

History of the tool

I developed the COACH tool as an enhancement of the GROW model currently in widespread use in the coaching world. Sir John Whitmore was an early author to record and popularize the GROW approach. The model, however, has been criticized for lacking a stage wherein the coaching topic is clarified; the rather cumbersome TO GROW acronym was developed to get around this limitation. The addition of the necessity to create a hard copy action plan adds a useful degree of accountability, whereby the coach and coachee are very clear on what has to be done, by whom and by when.

Related tools

1. GOLD tool – see Chapter 2, page 15.
2. STORM goals – see Chapter 3, page 29.
3. STAGES feedback – see Chapter 4, page 45.

Further reading

1. Greene, Jane and Grant, Anthony M. (2003) *Solution-focused Coaching: Managing People in a Complex World*. Momentum (Paperback: 192 pages; ISBN: 184304028X).
2. Whitmore, John (1996) *Coaching for Performance*, 2nd edition. Nicholas Brealey (Paperback; ISBN: 1857881702).
3. Downey, Myles (1995) *Effective Coaching*, 3rd edition. Orion (Paperback; ISBN: 0925652032).

Learning points summary

- Follow the COACH sequence, using appropriate questioning.
- The questions help learners think through the problem for themselves, clarify their understanding and arrive at their own solutions.
- A coach does not have to be a subject expert (this can be a disadvantage, as it may lead to giving advice) – he or she is a facilitator.
- Learning how to structure their thinking for one issue will help coachees to do it for themselves in the future.

Take Action!

Write down your thoughts on follow-up coaching; what you will do in your next session with the COACH tool.

Use the model to coach yourself and write down your thought process.

Choose a topic you are having difficulty with and can learn from. (*Clue*: It's probably happening today!)

- Use the COACH sequence as often as necessary in one coaching conversation.
- You may not need to spend time exploring the problem – if the issues are clear, as they were in our examples, focus on solutions.
- Sometimes just talking through an issue can bring about change.
- You may have to be creative and think about the issue from another angle. Using the 'miracle question' or getting the coachee to focus on what a good job looks like with someone else at the centre (another chairperson in our example) are two ways of doing this.
- As a coach, you not only engage in talking the issues through, you are also modelling good practice.
- If you don't have time in a session to tackle all the issues, get the coachee to prioritize them, focus on each one in order of priority, make a note of the others and make sure you arrange a time to finish the discussion and follow up. Keep motivation up and don't let the ball roll into the long grass!
- Use the GOLD model to follow up and review action points.

www.CoachingToolbook.com

Visit **www.CoachingToolbook.com** for a downloadable version of the COACH tool.

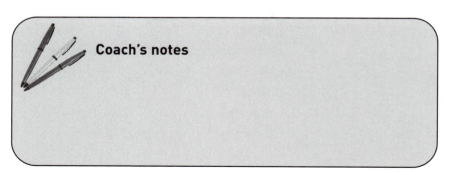

Coach's notes

Following up on a coaching session

Helping others learn from experience and behave in new ways – a tool worth its weight in GOLD!

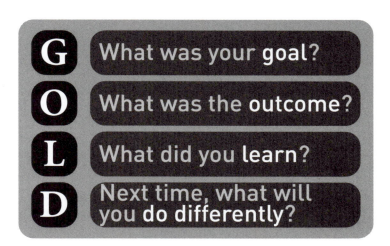

G What was your **goal**?

O What was the **outcome**?

L What did you **learn**?

D Next time, what will you **do differently**?

Visit:
www.CoachingToolbook.com

One of your team has done something, either as a result of your earlier coaching or independently. Chances are it won't have been 100 per cent successful and, as a coaching manager, you're keen to ensure that the person learns from their experience. Here's where a quick conversation can really help improve performance for next time, by reflecting on what's happened this time. The questions and prompts you give might seem simple – and they are – but the beauty of this technique is that you're helping your team to think it all through for themselves. This way they will get the best outcome – and so will you.

It is possible your team member will come for a chat after an event, in which case you'll be ready with the right things to say. If not, then it's well worth making the time to follow up. It will only take minutes but the benefits will be far reaching.

When to use this tool

⇒   After a previous coaching conversation (see COACH tool in Chapter 1).
⇒   After an assigned task.
⇒   When someone comes for help on action/s they have taken.

How to use the tool

This is a useful tool to guide you through a conversation which is focused on reflecting upon and extracting the most that can be learned from an experience. It is most valuable as a follow up when your coachee has returned following a significant action step – an 'experience'. So, what next? Remember, a key component to success in coaching is experience and learning over time. Follow up is critical. You will take the coachee through a sequence of questions to help them learn from their experience, i.e. probing through questioning, clarifying understanding and then creating new options.

> Do not believe that possibly you can escape the reward of your action.
>
> *Ralph Waldo Emerson (1803–1882), writer and public speaker*

Sample coaching conversation

Follow the four stages of the GOLD sequence as the coachee seeks to understand and learn from a presentation given that morning. Note that the outcome is a series of action steps to build skills and deepen learning for future success.

Coachee: Hey, coach. I did the presentation this morning and I would really appreciate a little more coaching.

Manager: Sure. First things first. **What were the goals** for your presentation?

Coachee: Well, two main things. First, I wanted to be less nervous than I was for the last presentation I did – I stuttered and stammered for 20 minutes. And secondly, I wanted to handle any questions at the end with confidence.

Manager: Composure and calm during the delivery, and confidence during the questioning.

Coachee: That's right.

Manager: Tell me, **what went well** this morning?

Coachee: I did pretty well handling the questions. I mean, I have been running the project for three months and know the details. I think that came across in my answers. Two of my team members also gave me very positive feedback on how I managed the Q&A.

Manager: And **what didn't go so well** today?

Coachee: I was still very nervous. I felt unprepared for the delivery, especially during the first four or five minutes, still got my words wrong and my voice sounded very weak. I fluffed the first sentence and that really threw me off – took me a while to recover.

Manager: OK, mixed results. I'm wondering **what you learned** from today's experience?

Coachee: I guess that preparation is everything. And getting the opening right would set me up to continue in a strong way too.

Manager: Anything else?

Coachee: The more presentations I do, the better I will be.

Manager: Sounds like some things you could capture in your learning journal! Do you have another presentation coming up?

Coachee: Yeah, in two weeks' time.

Manager: So, **what will you do differently next time**?

Coachee: I am going to practise with a couple of people from my team at least twice before the next one. And I need to practise the first few lines many more times than that.

Manager: Anything else?

Coachee: Yes, I want to practise in front of the whole team of 12 people, and get them to give me feedback a couple of days before the real thing. Then I can make any changes, as needed.

Manager: My work here is done! Write down those action points and we can review again after your next presentation.

Unpacking the conversation

Now, read on for an analysis of the conversation in more depth.

In our example, the coachee returned following delivery of an important presentation to the senior members of the project team, and asked the manager coach for some more help. For the manager, armed with the GOLD tool, this was no problem. The coach began by asking about the goals of the presentation, i.e. what were the specific objectives (for more on setting goals, see the STORM tool in Chapter 3). The coach confirmed understanding of the goals with a simple summarizing statement: 'Composure and calm during the delivery, and confidence during the questioning.'

Next, the coach wanted to clarify the outcome related to those goals with the powerful questioning duo of what went well and what did not go well. It is helpful to ask the learner if their objectives were met or, if not, what partial goals were achieved. In this example, the coachee did a good job on the Q&A session, but lacked confidence delivering the presentation itself.

Our coachee was now asked about what they learned from this experience. Don't just be happy with one answer – feel free to squeeze for additional insights beyond the obvious. (What else did you learn? And something else?)

Take Action!

Emotions = learning. You are hard-wired to lay down memories in times of emotion.

Memories change behaviour, which changes performance.

Grab a Post-it note and put this gem on your monitor screen right now!

Note: In generating new behaviours, it is the experience and emotions that drive the change. The GOLD tool is most useful when applied hot on the heels of a meaningful task when emotions are engaged (but not overwhelming). Here you have a chance for true learning and not just intellectual musing.

Our manager coach was now positioned nicely to use the fourth stage of the tool by asking what they will do differently next time:

Manager: So, **what will you do differently next time**?

Coachee: I am going to practise with a couple of people from my team at least twice before the next one. And I need to practise the first few lines many more times than that.

Manager: Anything else?

The learner produced two options to overcome these difficulties next time. The coach pushed again with the useful phrase, 'Anything else?'

What you are actually doing here is moving into the last part of the COACH tool (see Chapter 1, page 1). By asking what the coachee will do differently, you are eliciting options and may close by asking, specifically, what they will do the next time around (what, when, where, etc.).

Note: Even if you have no content expertise or special knowledge relating to the topic, you can still add value by taking the learner through the GOLD sequence, just as you can coach effectively with the COACH process despite blissful ignorance of the subject matter. Sure, a little perspective helps, but it doesn't preclude your ability to improve the coachee's learning.

Second coaching conversation

Read the following example of a coaching dialogue and identify the GOLD structure used by our manager coach. Notice how the coach uses open questions exclusively, both to gather information and to stimulate more in-depth responses:

Coachee: Our coaching session last month on how I can learn to delegate more was very helpful, although I am still having some problems. Could we review that together now?

Manager: Absolutely. Let's refresh ourselves on what your objective was.

Coachee: I needed to delegate more report writing to two of my team members, to free up my own time for departmental planning.

Manager: OK. Could you be more specific? **(Probing question to find out more)**

Coachee: Well, our weekly sales forecasts took the most time and I asked Jim to take that on, and Susan was to do the productivity report.

Manager: What was the result? **(Open question)**

Coachee: Susan had done some work before on the productivity side and was up to speed fairly quickly. I had to spend two hours with her to fill in the gaps, and I was pleased with the quality of her work.

Manager: And how did Jim perform with the sales forecasts? **(Open question)**

Coachee: Jim had reassured me that he was familiar with the format needed and would liaise with sales to get the data. However, there were so many problems with the report that we spent the better part of two days trying to get things right. Jim was really quite demoralized with the whole process.

Manager: So you have effectively freed up time with Susan doing the productivity report, but you have used a lot of time with Jim and still haven't moved things forward. **(Summarizing statement)** What have you learned from this? **(Open question)**

Coachee: I have found Susan willing and competent to do more report production, and I think I will be able to increase her responsibilities further. However, while Jim is very capable, the sales forecasts are complicated and, in retrospect, I delegated too big a task. He was overwhelmed.

Manager: So what will you do differently next time? **(Open question)**

Coachee: I will break down large tasks into smaller units that I can then allocate. I will take more time to assess who I am delegating to and make sure there is a good match of skills to tasks.

Manager: Anything else?

Coachee: People need to be stretched to some degree, but I stretched Jim too far! I think I'll take a more active role in the early stages after delegation, to make sure people aren't pushed too far outside of their comfort zone.

Manager: Great. If you like, let's talk again next month and we can see how things have progressed. **(Keeping the momentum and motivation up by showing continued interest)**

Coachee: Thanks, I'd appreciate that.

Take Action!

Write something now – your thoughts on follow-up coaching or what you will do in your next coaching session with the GOLD tool.

Plan to use the model on yourself to review your own learning.

Where next?

Using the above example, what does the coach do next? Remember, it's the repetition and consistency of the coaching approach that helps make it effective. Once the coachee has produced some workable options for what he or she will do differently next time, the coach can then help the learner to be more specific.

The coachee in our example said that she would delegate smaller projects, consider the match between the delegated task and the experience, skills and capabilities of the person more carefully, and spend time with that person in the early stages of the task. You can say 'Great, do you have another task in mind?' and you may be able to help plan the delegation process there and then. Alternatively, you could arrange another meeting or get them to send you a rough plan for another delegation project via email. Ask, 'When can you send it to me? It will help me plan my schedule to have a look through before we meet.' You are then creating a short-term objective or a milestone for the coachee. You get the idea.

Take Action!

Help the coachee to break the learning project down into chunks with shorter-term objectives within the long-term goals.

Keep up the momentum and motivation by staying interested and signalling that you are there to help.

Set a date/time to talk together again. Simply agreeing on the next meeting helps with motivation and accountability. You're not there to threaten them with a big stick, but a gentle prompt can be what they most need.

The GOLD tool allows the coachee to learn for themselves, which is better than just being told what to do.

> Spoon-feeding in the long run teaches us nothing but the shape of the spoon.
>
> *E.M. Forster (1878–1970), British writer*

History of the tool

I have based the GOLD tool on David Kolb's well-known four-stage cycle depicting how adults learn from experience. Put very simply, the Kolb cycle is:

1. Having an experience.
2. Reflecting on it.
3. Understanding it.
4. Putting the learning into practice.

Bright Idea!

Do you know what your learning preference is? Have a guess – you probably don't need a questionnaire to get it right. Just think about your usual approach to new learning.

Peter Honey and Alan Mumford developed this four-stage cycle further and produced an inventory of learning style preferences to help individuals assess their own style. Most people learn in a combination of the following ways:

- Activist learners – like to learn new things, in the here and now, with other people, and are enthusiastic and want to have a go.
- Reflective learners – like to learn by thinking about things, often by themselves, and want to mull things over.
- Theorist learners – like to know the context, be sure that it is conceptually sound, structure their learning and want to know all about it.
- Pragmatist learners – like to apply the learning as soon as possible, to know that it works in practice and to get on with it.

Related tools

1. COACH tool – see Chapter 1, page 1.
2. STORM tool – see Chapter 3, page 29.
3. STAGES feedback – see Chapter 4, page 45.

Further reading

1. Honey, Peter (1995) *Learning Styles Questionnaire: Facilitator Guide*, 3rd edition. Human Resource Development (Paperback; ISBN: 0925652032).
2. Honey, Peter and Mumford, Alan (1989) *Capitalizing on Your Learning Style*. Human Resource Development (Paperback; ISBN: 0925652024).
3. Starr, Julie (2002) *The Coaching Manual: The Definitive Guide to the Process and Skills of Personal Coaching*. Prentice Hall (Paperback; ISBN: 0273661930).

Learning points summary

- ■ Use the GOLD model to review learning and to follow up on any significant experience.
- ■ Take the time to follow up your team members' learning events, even if they do not approach you.
- ■ Use it formally, in a learning review session, or informally, as a 'wash-up' chat.

- Show an interest in your team members' development to keep the momentum and motivation going.
- The focus is on reflecting upon an experience, understanding it and putting the learning into practice next time.
- Use open questions to elicit information and stimulate in-depth, specific responses.
- Ask the magic questions: 'What went well?' 'What didn't go so well?' and 'What did you learn?'
- Ask for specific examples of what did not go so well to generate action points.
- Remember the useful question, 'Anything else?'
- Remember that you can use this tool again and again to review and keep track of your coachee's progress.

Take Action!

It is well worth finding out your learning style as a manager, as it will help you to understand your coachee's point of view.

Visit **www.CoachingToolbook.com** for a downloadable version of the GOLD tool.

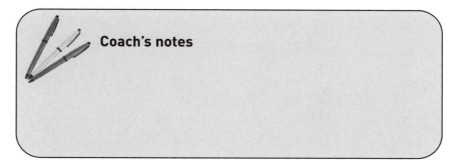

Coach's notes

Setting goals with a plan built in

The calm after this STORM is because you know what you want and where you're going

S Specific result

T Time to complete

O Others who can help

R Resources needed

M Measure of progress

Visit:
www.CoachingToolbook.com

This tool is useful and workmanlike. It is invaluable for setting objectives and getting the action going to achieve them. It helps you and your coachees to set a well-defined objective and identify the people and resources you need to set it in motion. This distinguishes it from other objective setting models, as the STORM process itself generates your first action steps towards achieving it – an objective setting and action planning tool in one!

When to use this tool

⇒ Any time you need to set an objective, identify the resources and people you need to get started.

⇒ To help someone specify and refine a general outcome.

⇒ In conjunction with the COACH model.

How to use the tool

This is a simple and practical tool that you can use in any situation. We all need to set goals, perhaps just for that day or week, or longer-term goals that are strategically important to us.

The model has two parts. First, it allows you to plan exactly where you want to go and when you want to arrive, and second, how you will get there. You can see the similarity to the principle behind the coaching conversations found in Chapter 1 (COACH tool).

The first two steps help you and your coachee to define your objective. You will need to identify the **specific result** by asking the magic question, 'What will it look like?' Next, you will have to help your coachee to decide on the **time by when it will be completed**.

The next steps are to identify **others who can help** in reaching the objective and the **resources needed**. This gives your coachee the first action steps with which to get started. Finally, there needs to be a **measure of progress** for where he or she has got to and for verifying the result.

> An average person with average talents and ambition and average education, can outstrip the most brilliant genius in our society, if that person has clear, focused goals.
>
> *Mary Kay Ash (1918–2001),*
> *US businesswoman and founder of Mary Kay Cosmetics*

Sample coaching conversation

This example shows how the STORM model can be used to set a sound development objective during a performance review. Jan is a team leader whose manager is helping him to set and define a clear objective around his communication skills with his team:

Jan: Hi. Have you got a few minutes? Can you help me think through how I can get my team communicating and working together more? Everyone is working on his or her own thing, and there's no sense of the team as a unit.

Manager: Of course. Can you be more **specific about the result you're after**?

Jan: This is where I got stuck myself. My goal, to get them working as a team, seems a bit wishy-washy.

Manager: OK. Ideally, what would things look like, what would you actually see, if the team was working together well?

Jan: (Thinks, looking pained.) I wish I could see it, but I can't.

Manager: OK. Take a step back. Imagine you're a stranger who's just walked in. What would be happening?

Jan: That's easier. There'd be a buzz. People would be talking to each other – maybe a couple of people standing up, talking about work. A couple of people leaning over a monitor. Projects would be moving on – purpose. Motivation.

Manager: So, it's energetic. Work focused. Purposeful. People working together. I've written that down. Anything else?

Jan: Our team meetings would have energy. We'd be involved with each other.

Manager: You've just mentioned team meetings. Would you see all of these things in a team meeting?

Jan: Yes.

Manager: That narrows it down.

Jan: Yes. I think that's a good starting point.

Manager: Good. Now let's put it all together and write it down as if it's happening now. Start with, 'The team meeting is...'

Jan: OK. (Pause as he writes.) I've got, 'The team meeting is buzzing. There's energy and purpose. People are involved with each other, motivated and talking.' Yes.

Manager: Fine. That's your specific result. Now. **When do you want to achieve that?**

Take Action!

Think of an area of your own life where you need to set a goal, e.g. finance, career, health.

Write a small, quick-win STORM goal right now and stick it on your fridge!

Jan: I think three months would be realistic.

Manager: OK. So let's look at a date three months from now. December?

Jan: Yes. I've written it down. December 1st.

Manager: Now let's look at **who will help you do this**.

Jan: Team members, obviously. You, as my coach.

Manager: Anyone else?

Jan: No. I can't think of anyone else.

Manager: OK. Write down the names of the specific team members who can help, and me.

Jan: OK. (Writes it down.)

Manager: **What resources would you need?** Time? Equipment? Budget?

Jan: Time, yes. Not more time – different time. We have meetings already. And my commitment. Nothing else.

Manager: **How would you measure your progress?** How will you know that it has worked?

Jan: It will have worked when I walk into a team meeting that has energy, buzz and involvement.

Manager: Are there any milestones that will tell you that you're getting there?

Jan: Yes. When team members are ready for the meeting, interested in it and want to get started.

Manager: So that's our first measure of progress. We can move on from there. I think we've got our objective. Let's look at how you can get your resources and people together, as a couple of initial action points. We may need another session to work out an action plan.

Jan: I've been thinking about it as we've talked. I could put it to the team and ask for their help. What do you think?

Manager: Excellent. Any other thoughts on that?

Jan: I'm thinking fresh and different – our team meetings are always on Tuesday mornings. I could scrap next week's meeting and call one at a different time. That would make it different. Then I could ask them how we could do it. Put my ideal result on the table and ask for their ideas. What do you think?

Manager: Great. You've got an action point. Let's make a date to review.

Unpacking the example

Learning Point

Man is a goal-seeking animal. His life only has meaning if he is reaching out and striving for his goals.

Aristotle

Jan has approached the manager coach with an idea that he says is wishy-washy. He knows what he's after but needs to make it more concrete. He is having trouble expressing it. He and the coach spend some time pinning down the ideal result. First, the coach gets him to visualize it, asking what it would look like. This question doesn't quite work, as Jan can't 'see' it. It may be that he doesn't imagine things visually – occasionally people find it easier to imagine in terms of what is happening, what it feels like or maybe even what it sounds like. It may also be that it's too early in the process. He may need to think around the desired result before stating it specifically.

If this question doesn't work, don't worry. Try another angle. In this example, our coach prompts him to step back and imagine he's a stranger. He asks, 'What would be happening?' which generates a lot of ideas. (This method is called the 'miracle question' and derives from solution-focused behaviour change, as popularized by the therapists Steve de Shazer and Insoo Kim Berg.)

Manager: OK. Ideally, what would things look like, what would you actually see, if the team was working together well?

The coach then picks up on the team meeting as a specific event to focus on. Jan agrees. The coach asks him to write it down as if it's happening now, and gives him the beginning of his sentence: 'The team meeting is. . .'. This makes it immediate and real. Eventually, Jan comes up with a specific result.

In the next part of the conversation, the coach asks him when he wants to achieve it by, and Jan thinks that 1 December – in three months' time – would be a good time for completion. This wraps up the first phase of a STORM goal – where to and by when.

The coach then moves the conversation on to the second STORM phase (the way in which Jan will reach the goal) by asking about the people who can help, and Jan comes up with the coach and his team members. The coach asks, 'Anyone else?' to get him to think more about it, but Jan says 'No'. Then the coach asks about resources and gives some examples to help. Jan thinks he needs time, but not more time, just a different use of time, and his own commitment. He doesn't need any more resources. They move on to how to measure progress:

Manager: How would you measure your progress? How will you know that it has worked?

Jan defines his final measure. The coach asks about milestones on the way – what will tell him that he's getting there – and Jan clearly identifies this first measure.

As the conversation progresses, Jan has thought of a first step, prompted by the questions about others who can help. The process has given him his first action step. They plan to review this and he's on his way. You can use the COACH model, if needed, to expand options and drill down on action steps.

Second coaching conversation

The second example conversation shows how the STORM model can help with longer-term personal objectives. The following dialogue is the beginning of a career development meeting that Miriam has initiated to talk about her Personal Development Plan (PDP) with the Training and Development Manager. Miriam is a manager who wants to get on and doesn't mess about!

Manager: So, Miriam, you've asked to talk to me about your PDP; what you want out of your career, how you can get there and how we can help you. Before we look at what you will do tomorrow, let's look at your longer-term objectives – where you want to be in five years' time. Is that OK?

Miriam: I don't want to look too far into the future. Can we start with my one-year objectives? I can see one year ahead. I can't see five years in advance.

Manager: OK. So what do you want to be doing in a year's time? **(Specific outcome)**

Miriam: I know that exactly. My boss will be retiring then – so I hear. I want her job.

Manager: Well, that's clear enough! And now I see why you wanted to talk to me first – normally it's line manager first, then us. But this is fine. Does it have to be that particular job?

Miriam: Maybe not. That one seems to be realistic – I can see it happening. I know she thinks I'm good. But any job at that level would do!

Manager: I'll write down 'Department Manager'. And you want that to be at the end of one year? **(Time to complete)**

Miriam: Yes. That seems a reasonable timescale. This time next year.

Manager: OK. Let's look at who can help you to achieve it. Any ideas? **(Others who can help. Open question)**

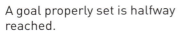

Learning Point

A goal properly set is halfway reached.
Abraham Lincoln

Miriam: Obviously, my boss can help me. Then you can help me with training and development. I'd also like a mentor. Would that be possible? I know there's a company mentoring scheme.

Manager: I'll have to find out about a mentor for you, and I'll get back to you on that. It would have to go through your boss, of course. I'll write 'mentor' down. And I've got your boss and myself. Anyone else? **(Drilling down for more ideas)**

Miriam: I can't think of anyone at the moment. I do know that my boss is the most important person.

Manager: Good. What about resources? Do you need anything else? **(Resources needed. Open question)**

Miriam: I've thought about more training – I've really got to get to grips with budgeting and financial management. And I think I need to know more about policy and how a department works.

Manager: Good. I'll make a note of the financial training. We have courses running on financial management, and I can get you on the next one if you like. Speak to your boss – she has to sign it off. I suggest that you'll need to go on the leadership course, too. Again, you'll have to have the conversation with your boss about that. OK. How can you access information on policy and how a department works, do you think? **(Encourages her to think about opportunities)**

Miriam: That's down to her, too, I think. I need to get involved in meetings and get access to policy information. I realize that I'll have to get her on board.

Manager: That sounds good – it looks as if she's your main ally, if she's willing. I'll underline 'Speak to boss'. Now, let's look at how you'll measure your progress. First, I want to write down how you will know you've achieved your objective. And before you say, 'I'll have her job,' think about what would happen if she doesn't retire. What if that job isn't up for grabs? **(Hypothesizing question)**

Miriam: OK. I'll be a Department Manager.

Manager: Now, let's look at how you will know that you're getting there. What will you be doing in three months' time, six months' time and nine months' time? Start with three months' time, and be as specific as you can. **(Measure of progress)**

Miriam: OK. In three months' time, I'll have my boss on my side, I'll have a mentor. I'll have been on the financial management course.

Manager: Good. And in six months' time? **(Establishing milestones)**

Miriam: Hopefully I'll have started on the leadership course. I'll be attending department meetings and taking on higher level projects.

Manager: OK. Got that. In nine months?

Miriam: By then, my boss will be starting to hand over.

Manager: Great. That's that tied up, then! We'll need to plan exactly how you'll do those things, so we need to talk about that. We've got a few action points so far. Shall I summarize?

Miriam: Yes.

Bright Idea!

Download the STORM worksheet from www.CoachingToolbook.com

Manager: OK. Actions for you. Most important – make an appointment to talk to your boss about your plans. Also, ask her about the mentor, financial training, leadership training, taking on higher level projects, learning about policy and how a department works. My actions are to find out about dates for financial management courses, info on the leadership course and about a mentor. Have you got anything I haven't mentioned? **(Clarifies the communication and understanding)**

Miriam: I think that's it.

Manager: Good. Give me a call when you've talked to your boss and tell me how it goes. Email me when you've booked a date to talk to her, so I'll be waiting! Good luck!

Where next?

Once you have identified a clear, action-oriented objective with the STORM model, you will need to use the GOLD model to review and measure your coachee's progress on an ongoing basis. You may also want to use it at the beginning of the COACH model (O – Outcome desired), and work through the steps to develop and explore the action planning process in more depth.

History of the tool

The STORM tool is a refinement of the SMART (Specific, Measurable, Achievable, Realistic, Time-bound) model for objective setting, which has found to be awkward to use at times. There can be confusion about the difference between achievable and realistic in the SMART model, and the author also wanted a tool that was more practical and action oriented.

SMART is focused on defining the objective itself, without pointers as to how to achieve it. STORM not only helps users to identify the specific result they are looking for, with a completion time point and an observable measure of progress, but also helps them towards achieving it. The structure of a STORM conversation is firmly based on the coaching methodology of 'where am I now; where do I want to go; how and when will I get there?' as seen in how to hold a coaching conversation in Chapter 1 (COACH tool).

Related tools

1. COACH tool – see Chapter 1, page 1.
2. GOLD tool – see Chapter 2, page 15.
3. OPERA tool – see Chapter 6, page 79.

Further reading

1. Greene, Jane and Grant, Anthony M. (2003) *Solution-focused Coaching: Managing People in a Complex World.* Momentum (Paperback: 192 pages; ISBN: 184304028X).
2. Tracy, Brian (2003) *Goals! How to Get Everything You Want, Faster Than You Ever Thought Possible.* Berrett-Koehler, USA (Hardcover: 250 pages; ISBN: 1576752356).
3. Rouillard, Larrie (2002) *Goals and Goal Setting: Achieving Measured Objectives.* Crisp Publications Inc. (Paperback: 106 pages; ISBN: 1560526777).

Learning points summary

Take Action!

Use the STORM tool on your-self to create a clear forward-looking objective. Find out how well it works.

- STORM gives you and your coachees a tool to help set a well-defined, time-bounded objective, which also helps you to identify the people and resources needed to set it in motion.
- The process of identifying people and resources needed to achieve the objective generates the first steps of an action plan.
- Use it at the beginning of the COACH model.
- Use the GOLD model to review your coachees' progress towards their objective on an ongoing basis, using the measurements of progress you have already identified.

Visit **www.CoachingToolbook.com** for a downloadable version of the STORM tool.

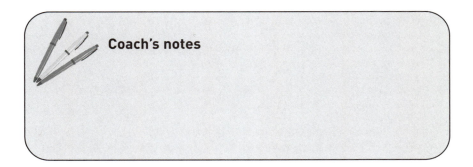

Coach's notes

Giving feedback that works

Make sure your feedback can be easily swallowed and digested – give it in STAGES!

S	Setting
T	Topic of feedback
A	Ask for opinion
G	Give feedback
E	Establish action plan
S	Set review date

Visit:
www.CoachingToolbook.com

We all know that feedback is a good thing – people only learn from experience if they know what they did and how they did it. We know that we need to give it and ask for it. Despite that, it is surprising how hard it is to give well – so that the person on the other end of it understands it, accepts it and acts on it – and how easily it can go wrong. Feedback is important, and it will be more effective if it's given at the right time, in the right place and from one adult to another rather than as a parent to a naughty child. If it is clumsily given, as criticism without discussion, it will not work and may indeed have the opposite effect. Read this chapter to find out how to give constructive and highly effective feedback.

When to use this tool

⇒ Any time you need to give feedback.

⇒ When you are helping someone to learn.

⇒ When someone asks for your opinion on something they have done.

⇒ When you need to give constructive feedback to a team member on their behaviour or a piece of work.

How to use the tool

STAGES is a tool that you can use in any situation where you are giving feedback – whether it's having a timely word with a team member, in a more formal environment like a review (see Chapter 8) or as part of a learning event.

The first part of the STAGES model is getting the **setting** right, both physically and emotionally. If either of these is wrong, the person on the other end of it will not be able to take the feedback on board and may be very upset by it, however well intentioned you may be. You then need to outline the **topic**, so that he or she knows what it is about. Next, you need to **ask for the person's own opinion** of their work or behaviour. More often than not, he or she will be aware of any shortcomings (if the feedback is negative) and will be able to evaluate their actions themselves. Whether or not they are aware, this is the best place to start. After that, you **give the feedback**, making sure it's specific and usable (a reminder of how to give helpful and specific feedback can be found on page 52 of this chapter).

The final parts of the conversation are to **establish an action plan** and to **set a review date**. For true learning to take place, the feedback should typically be followed by new and different behaviour. Without a hard copy action plan and a definite review date, you have just been having a conversation. You can see the connection to the basic coaching idea – where you are now and where you need to be (ask for their opinion and give the specific feedback), and work out how you will get there (establish an action plan and review date). Notice the similarity to the COACH model in Chapter 1.

> It is impossible for a man to learn what he thinks he already knows.
>
> *Epictetus (c55–c135 CE), philosopher*

Sample coaching conversation

Our manager coach has just overheard a phone conversation that Mike was having with a customer. He's at his desk in an open plan office. She taps him on the shoulder:

Manager: Mike, do you have time for a chat in my office?

Mike: Yeah, sure. (They go into the office, where they will not be disturbed or overheard by other team members: **the physical setting**. The **emotional setting** is informal and not heavy handed.)

Manager: I've just heard your side of the conversation with one of our customers. **(The topic)**

Mike: Oh. Right.

Manager: How do you think it went? **(Asks for Mike's opinion)**

> **Mike:** Not good. She was angry and sarcastic and I was losing my patience. I could have lost my rag, but I didn't. It all ended OK.
>
> **Manager:** I heard you saying that it wasn't your fault, blaming the back office for the problem and saying that there's nothing you can do. She must have felt even more frustrated and angry. It's not like you; you're usually good with complaints. **(Gives feedback)** Can you comment on that? **(Asks for opinion again)**

Learning Point

If you want to truly understand something, try to change it.
  Kurt Lewin

Mike: Like I said, she was having a go at me – and it was down to the back office people. Yes, I know I shouldn't have said what I did, but I had had it up to here.

Manager: OK. I realize how difficult it is to deal with complaints about our service when other parts of the company mess

Coachee: I could – and I know I should – apologize for the inconvenience and say I'll look into it for her.

Manager: Good. Now can you say exactly what you would say in that situation, but to me?

Mike: (Pauses to think.) I'm sorry this has happened and I understand that it's put you to a lot of trouble. I'll contact the office and find out what has happened and ring you back, if that's all right.

Manager: Great! I'll write those words down now to remind you. **(Establish an action plan)** Could you do anything else to help yourself when you begin to lose patience?

Mike: I suppose I could take a break if I begin to get irritated. Maybe get it off my chest by talking to someone?

Manager: Sounds sensible. I'll write those down too.

Mike: OK. It was a one-off, you know.

Manager: Yes, I know, Mike, and that's why I wanted a word with you now. Here's what I've written down. Let's talk again tomorrow at the same time. **(Set review date)**

Unpacking the example

Bright Idea!

Download the STAGES worksheet from www.Coaching Toolbook.com

In this example, the manager chose to give feedback as soon as Mike came off the phone. Her request to have a chat was informal but direct. She made sure that it took place in her office, where they would not be overheard or interrupted and where she could give him her full attention. Giving this kind of feedback in front of Mike's colleagues would have been embarrassing for him and would have made it more of an issue than it needed to be. (The emotional and physical setting was appropriate for the task.)

Manager: Mike, do you have time for a chat in my office?

She then outlined the topic, so that he was clear what it was about. Next, she asked for his opinion of what had happened. He had been aware that his response was inappropriate, and said so. It can be very helpful to ask for the coachee's opinion first, as they may already have learned the lesson you are about to give. It will help alleviate the frequent anxiety associated with the statement, 'Can I see you in my office?' (Also, humans have a culture of reciprocal behaviour – you have had your turn and now it is mine. Having asked for their opinion first means your feedback is more likely to be heard and received.)

She then gives her feedback, being specific about what she had heard, telling him the effect it would have had and letting him know that she appreciated that this was not what happened normally:

Manager: I heard you saying that it wasn't your fault, blaming the back office for the problem and saying that there's nothing you can do. She must have felt even more frustrated and angry. It's not like you, you're usually good with complaints. **(Gives feedback)** Can you comment on that? **(Asks for opinion again)**

She knew that he was aware that his response had been unreasonable, and she asked him to comment on it, which he did. Then she asked him what he would do differently. She sympathized with his situation, and asked him what he could say next time, as if she were the customer. She then

Bright Idea!

When we fail to prepare, we prepare to fail.

Help your coachee to have a solid plan to prepare for a learning opportunity.

wrote that down as an action point, establishing an action plan, which she built on, asking him if there was anything else he could do to prevent it happening again. His reply – that he would take a break when he knew he was getting irritated and talk to someone else about it – became the second point of the action plan, which she noted and gave him. She then suggested that they talk again at the same time the next day, thus setting a review date.

Ten steps to giving good feedback

Take some time to read through the following key points on giving feedback, before you read the next sample conversation:

1. Give it at the right time – as soon as possible after the event. However, if the event is emotionally loaded (i.e. if either you or the team member is angry or upset), wait until the situation has settled, but not too long.
2. Don't make it into a drama if it isn't one – match your approach to the importance of the issue.
3. Give feedback in a conversation – adult to adult.
4. Don't save it up and give it all at once – it makes the experience more unpleasant and the individual will not be able to take it all in.
5. Feedback should be between you and the other person. Never give feedback to someone in public or in front of his or her colleagues. Find somewhere private, where you will not be interrupted, and give the individual your full attention and enough time.

6. Focus on the behaviour and don't get personal. Be specific about what you have observed.
7. Say what the effects of the behaviour were (or could be).
8. Say why it is not acceptable, if necessary.
9. If you can honestly give the individual some positive feedback, do so, but beware of the 'praise sandwich' effect: 'I think you're really great at your job, but...' It sounds insincere and undermines any real praise you might give in future.
10. Establish an action plan of what he or she could do differently next time. Follow it up and review as planned.

Visit **www.CoachingToolbook.com** for a downloadable version of these ten feedback points.

Second coaching conversation

The second example conversation is more formal. The manager has agreed to review a presentation given by the coachee, and they have already set aside half an hour (setting). The coachee, Leah, comes to the manager's office and the feedback session begins:

Manager: Hello. Sit down. So, we've got half an hour to review your presentation. **(Manager confirms the topic and how long they have)**

Leah: I'm dreading this!

Manager: Why? How do you think it went? **(Asks her opinion)**

Leah: I blew it. That's all.

Manager: Well, I was there too, and I didn't see that. I saw you run out of time at the end, though! **(Acknowledges the problem and the emotional temperature, but gives a calm, measured response)** Talk me through what went well. **(Encourages her to talk about it positively)**

Leah: I prepared it well, I think. I had everything ready, and my notes were comprehensive.

Manager: Yes, I could see that. What about the delivery? **(Specific open question to elicit more information)**

Leah: I started off well, I thought. I was hyped up on adrenaline, but I wasn't too nervous. I covered all the important points, and my PowerPoint slides looked good. But I lost track of time and when I looked at the clock, I saw I wasn't going to get everything in. Then I panicked and started to gabble and still didn't manage to cover the ground.

Manager: I agree with some of that. The first ten minutes were very good – you seemed sure of your arguments and put them well. You were really getting the hang of it. You covered all the most important points up front, and the slides were relevant and not too detailed. I saw you looking at the time, and then you took off at top speed! **(Gives feedback and encouragement)**

Leah: I know.

Manager: So what could you do differently to prevent that from happening again? **(Taken from the action planning of the GOLD tool)**

Leah: I know I should have rehearsed it properly beforehand. I did practise and time it, and I did a quick run-through with a colleague, but I didn't practise the whole thing as 'live' in front of anyone else.

Bright Idea!

Don't help your coachee to dwell on the problem – focus on what went well and move to a solution.

Manager: Yes. It would have helped. I'll make a note of that as an action point. **(Establish an action plan)** Anything else?

Leah: I know there were times when I went into too much detail. It was all there in the notes. Maybe I could have cut it, but I can't see how. What do you think?

Manager: I think you could have cut some of the detail. **(Gives more feedback)** Can you think of anything you could have done without? **(Open question to encourage exploration)**

Leah: Not really. I stated my argument up front, I sold the benefits to the people listening – and I did a lot of research on what they would be. Then I anticipated their possible objections.

Manager: Could you have done without that part – anticipating their objections? **(Makes a suggestion, building on Leah's earlier comment, as she has drawn a blank)**

Leah: Yes – I could have left that for the Q&A afterwards, couldn't I?

Manager: I think you could have done. Shall I put that down as an action point?

Leah: Yes. I think I could also do without so much detail when I was selling the benefits.

Manager: Another action point?

Leah: Yes. And now I'm thinking more clearly about it, I was wondering if I could have done something about it at the time.

Manager: You mean to rescue the situation? **(Restating to clarify and check understanding)** Go on. **(Encouraging her to express her thoughts)**

Learning Point

Too many action points can mean that none are followed through. Don't overwhelm your coachee with too much to work on. Three or four points per session is about right.

Leah: OK. Like, um... **(Pauses. Coach stays silent)** Well, I'm thinking that it was all there in my notes, which they had. Maybe I could have pointed that out.

Manager: Keep going.

Leah: When I was saying before about leaving the 'anticipating objections' bit for the Q&A. I could have just run through my last two slides – the 'benefits' and the 'objections' key points – then referred them to my notes and invited questions. I suppose I could have planned to do that. What do you think?

Manager: That sounds good to me. Shall I get those down as action points?

Leah: Yes. I can't think of anything else now.

Manager: OK. I think we've got enough to be going on with! I'll read back what I've got down on the action plan. **(Summarizes the points)** 1) Rehearse! 2) Cut out some of the detail. 3) Outline the benefits and potential objections only – show slides and refer listeners to the notes. 4) Invite listeners to question you. Does that sound right? **(Closed question to check understanding)**

Leah: Yes. I've got another presentation next month. I'll use these for that.

Manager: OK. Let's arrange a date before then to look at how your plans for that are going. **(Set review date)**

Where next?

Once you have generated some action steps together, you can use the GOLD model (Chapter 2, page 15) for follow up and review. This tool can also be incorporated into many of the other models in the book – for example, the COACH tool (Chapter 1), the DROPS tool (Chapter 5) and, of course, during a performance review using the second STAGES model (Chapter 8).

This tool ensures that the six key stages of feedback are included in any review discussion. Missing any one stage can mean the whole conversation can lose its effect on reflection and true behaviour change.

History of the tool

This tool has been developed by drawing on the author's own experience as an executive coach and coaching skills trainer. The model draws on a number of well-tried feedback techniques, such as paying attention to the physical and emotional setting before starting the process, which means that the feedback is more likely to be heard and acted on. Asking for the coachee's opinion before giving the feedback and drawing on their own experience and judgement means that the person is treated as an adult and makes giving feedback a two-way interaction. This starts off a process of reflection and learning from his or her actions.

Related tools

1. COACH tool – see Chapter 1, page 1.
2. GOLD tool – see Chapter 2, page 15.
3. STAGES for performance reviews – see Chapter 8, page 121.

Further reading

1. Smart, J. K. (2003) *Real Coaching and Feedback: How to Help People Improve Their Performance.* Prentice Hall (Paperback: 144 pages; ISBN: 0273663283).
2. Maurer, Rick (1995) *Feedback Toolkit: 16 Tools for Better Communication in the Workplace.* Productivity Press Inc. (Paperback: 109 pages; ISBN: 1563270560).

Learning points summary

- Feedback is important – it enhances how we learn from experience.
- Use the STAGES for feedback model in any situation where you need to give feedback – formally or informally.
- Make sure you approach the task appropriately, taking account of the situation and the receiver's state of mind.
- Give feedback as soon as possible after the event, and after any emotional overload has passed.
- Give the feedback in private.

- Give the person your full attention and make sure you will not be disturbed.
- Clearly identify the topic.
- Focus on observable and specific actions.
- Write down the action points as they arise and check that the receiver is committed to them.
- Review and follow up.

Take Action!

Ask for feedback on your own performance today – on anything you do. Write down the action points and use them!

Visit **www.CoachingToolbook.com** for a downloadable version of the STAGES feedback tool.

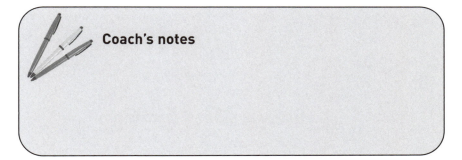

Coach's notes

How to find the best solution to a problem

Use this tool when a problem DROPS on to your desk!

D	Describe the problem
R	Reasons behind it
O	Options to solve it
P	Pros and cons of each
S	Select best option

Visit:
www.CoachingToolbook.com

A large part of a manager's job is to sort out problems in the workplace – their own, the business's, those of their team members. This tool is simple but effective and can be used in all kinds of situations and at all levels, from petty problems to overwhelming ones. It provides a logical sequence for unravelling the issues, weighing them up and arriving at a solution. It can also be used by team members individually, so that they can sort out their own problems – which means that you don't have to!

When to use this tool

⇒   Any time a team member comes to you with a problem.
⇒   For team members to use themselves to solve their own problems.
⇒   To resolve for yourself any problems you may face as a manager.

How to use the tool

When faced with a problem, the road ahead can sometimes be difficult to see clearly. We may simply turn to someone more experienced and ask for help, which is exactly what happened to Napoleon Bonaparte, the reported founder of the method. (See the 'History of the tool' later in this chapter for more details.)

The DROPS structure allows us to explore and understand a problem in more detail. The best solution can become apparent at any stage. For example, having completed the first step of fully describing the problem, the ideal way forward may become obvious.

The first step of this methodical approach to helping your team members to solve a challenging situation is to **describe the problem**. This is important – you may never arrive at the answer if you don't know what the question is in the first place, and this is not always as easy as it looks. You have to pinpoint exactly what you are dealing with.

Next, you need to explore the **reasons behind it**, to give you some background and paint a fuller picture. These reasons, when made clear, may reveal the optimal way forward. You then need to encourage your coachee to look at all the possible **options to solve it** – what they might do. You then encourage coachees to weigh up the **pros and cons of each** option. Finally, you help them to **select the best option**. Simple!

One useful way to use the tool when a direct report comes to you with a problem is to ask them to go away and perform a DROPS analysis on paper, and come back to you with their best option to resolve the issue. You can then talk through their notes, adding detail and perspective where needed.

> Fix the problem, not the blame.
>
> *Japanese proverb*

Sample coaching conversation

In this conversation, James, a new production manager, is having trouble with his supplier and he goes to his manager with the problem:

James: I've got a problem that I'd like to talk over with you. Do you have a few minutes?

Manager: Yes. What is it?

James: I'm having trouble with my supplier and I don't know what to do.

Manager: OK. **What exactly is the problem?** Take your time and explain it to me.

James: OK. It's DigiWorld – the digital printer. Since I've been in this job, they have let me down again and again. They've missed deadlines, and twice, they've made bad mistakes on exhibition panels. The first time it was the client who noticed it because DigiWorld said they always delivered direct, and anyway they were so close to the deadline that I had to say 'yes'. I noticed it myself the second time and was able to catch it, because I went down to their premises and checked the computer image before it went to print. I've always managed to get money back – after a fight! But it's not acceptable. The thing is, we've used them for years and my predecessor, Chris, thought they were great. They used to be our sole supplier, but that stopped a while ago, before I came, and we've been using another company as well. DigiWorld aren't able, or just can't be bothered, to handle all our stuff.

Manager: So DigiWorld are being unreliable. **Are there any specific reasons why?**

James: Well, it could be a number of things. I think that they respected Chris – he was really tough – and they're trying it on with me, putting our stuff to the back of the queue however early I get the order in. Then it could be that they resent the fact that they're no longer the sole supplier. The other thing is that I never speak to the same person

> ### Bright Idea!
>
> When looking for reasons behind the problem, you want to stay focused towards solutions.
>
> Some coachees will want to play the blame game. Try to move towards actual reasons for the problem.
>
> For more emotional situations, see the second coaching example in this chapter.

twice and messages aren't passed on. Chris had a good working relationship with the top guy, but I don't get to talk to him.

Manager: OK. Anything else?

James: Maybe it's because I don't nail everything down on the purchase order – but I don't think so. I am very careful to detail everything. I'd never have got our money back if I hadn't.

Manager: OK. So either they're trying it on with you because you're new and not as tough as Chris was, or you don't have a one-to-one relationship with someone with clout. Or they don't like the fact that we're using other companies – and maybe you don't nail the details down on the purchase orders. Is that right?

James: Yes.

Manager: OK. I've got the picture. Let's look at what you can do about it. **What are the options?** I'll write them down and we can look at the pros and cons afterwards.

James: Well, we could ditch them completely. Or we could give the important stuff to the other company, and ditch them gradually. Or I could get tougher with them. Or I could develop a relationship with someone there that I trust to get the job done.

Manager: Right. That's four. Any more?

James: No. Can't think of any more.

Manager: OK. **Let's look at the pros and cons of each option.** Number one is ditching them completely. What are the pros?

James: I wouldn't have to put up with their unreliability. I wouldn't have to put up with their sloppy attitude. I'd save myself the grief.

Manager: And the cons?

James: Well, I'm not sure the other company would be able to handle all our stuff. I'd have to find another digital print supplier to take some of it. Another supplier wouldn't be so familiar with the way we work, so I'd have to coach them along and build the relationship.

Manager: What about giving the more important stuff to the other company and easing DigiWorld out gradually? What are the pros?

James: The other company would be able to handle some of our stuff and maybe they would build up to handling the rest. But I can't help thinking of the cons.

Manager: Which are?

James: They will definitely know that we're easing them out, so they will get even sloppier.

Manager: What about getting tougher with them? Pros?

James: In theory, they wouldn't mess me about and things would get done.

Manager: Cons?

James: I'd have to change my style. I feel as if I'm in Chris's shadow and it's uncomfortable. He was just plain aggressive at times. He could be really threatening. I'm not the same animal.

Manager: What about four – developing a relationship with someone you trust to get the job done? Pros?

James: I'd get to talk to one person all the time. He or she would be responsible for the job.

Manager: Cons?

James: I don't know whom it would be or how to find the right person.

Manager: Anything else on pros and cons?

James: No. But things are falling into place. I came in here with a gut feeling that I had to get rid of DigiWorld completely. Now I'm not sure I can. I don't think it would be a good move and the implications could be disastrous.

Manager: I've written notes on the options with all the pros and cons. Take it with you if you need to think more about it. **Have you any thoughts on which option to go for?**

James: I think I will carry on giving some of the work to the other company, but continue to use DigiWorld. I really should try to develop a relationship with one of the people down there, so I need to think of ways of doing it. Could we have a session on that?

Manager: Yes, of course, but I've run out of time. What about Thursday at two o'clock?

James: Good for me. That will give me time to think some more about it. Thanks very much for this. I'll see you on Thursday.

Unpacking the example

James came to his manager coach with a problem he had been wrestling with for a while. The manager asks him to describe what is happening, giving him time to do it and listening carefully. It is not always easy to

Bright Idea!

When faced with a problem we can get confused or overwhelmed. The problem can run around in our heads.

Write down the problem as clearly as you can on a piece of paper, and then forget about it until the next day.

You may be surprised at how you now view that issue more clearly.

Try it for yourself!

get the facts straight in one go, particularly if coachees have had it going round and round in their heads. You may need to question and prompt to get to the heart of things.

In our example, James is well able to describe the situation. The coach understands from the description that the problem is DigiWorld's unreliability, and he asks James to tell him the reasons behind the problem:

Manager: So DigiWorld are being unreliable. **Are there any specific reasons why?**

James gives him three reasons, adding another possibility when prompted with the 'Anything else?' question. The manager coach then summarizes the reasons, checking his understanding with a closed question, 'Is that right?' .

> A series of open questions followed by a focused or clarifying question is a common sequence in coaching.

Next, the manager moves on to ask James to think of some options to solve it, and James thinks of four possible solutions with ease. He then moves on to ask James to list the pros and cons for each solution, prompting and guiding him through each:

Manager: OK. **Let's look at the pros and cons of each option.** Number one is ditching them completely. What are the pros?

At the end of this process, James says that thinking it through has helped things to fall into place. He says he started out with a gut feeling that he wanted to get rid of DigiWorld completely, but now he's not so sure. This often happens when you are using this tool – your coachees may be able to make a selection without having to read through your notes and reviewing the pros and cons of each option. However, sometimes they may not be able to make a selection straight away, so they can take the notes away and reflect upon the best choice.

Another way it can work is that the coachee finds a solution in a combination of the options they have generated. James selects the best option – to continue to use DigiWorld and to find someone with whom he can build a working relationship and be his single point of contact. At the same time, he would also give work to the other company.

He realizes that he needs to think through ways of making this happen, and he asks for a further coaching session. Meanwhile, he will think more about his solution. Many people will find that they already have the answers – the coaching process can simply reveal what was already there.

Second coaching conversation

Managers have to be able to sort out 'people problems'. In this sample conversation, Nadia has come to her manager for help. She has got a problem and it has clearly got her angry and upset. Follow the stages of the model for yourself, as the conversation progresses:

Nadia: I've got a problem and I don't know how to solve it, so here I am. It's really screwing me up. I didn't think I should come to you but I can't think how else to get round it. Can we keep this confidential?

Manager: Yes, of course. Tell me about it.

Nadia: It's about me and Rob. He's driving me nuts. I don't think I can work with him at all.

Manager: What's happened?

Nadia: Nothing – that's it. (Dramatically!) Nothing has happened. That's the problem.

Manager: Can you be a bit more specific? (Smiling.) **(Another phrasing for the coach to get the coachee to describe the problem)**

Nadia: As you know, Rob and I are supposed to be working on this project together – just him and me. We have to research it, do a survey, write a report and present it to senior management. We've only got six weeks and I can't get him to sit down with me to plan it. Just a moment ago he fobbed me off again!

Learning Point

It may take time to tease out the actual problem, especially if the person is angry or upset. Be patient and keep asking open questions.

Manager: So, what's behind this? I can see you're upset. **(Acknowledges the temperature)**

Nadia: Don't get me wrong – he's a nice guy, full of ideas, good fun. But I've never worked closely with him before and I'm already having trouble. We've had a few short discussions about the project and that's what has upset me. He thinks we've got loads of time, but he hasn't read the brief properly. He doesn't even know what it's about, for God's sake. He says we don't need to plan – we should just get on with it. I've read it through and started doing some research because if I don't, it won't get done.

Manager: OK. If you had to pin down just one reason for this, what would it be?

Nadia: He's not doing anything and I'm doing everything.

Manager: That sounds like blame to me. Isn't it rather one sided? **(Coach gently points out that she's blaming or exaggerating and being unreasonable, using a closed question)**

Nadia: Yes. Sorry. I'm so mad. I'd say the reason comes down to work styles. They don't match.

Manager: OK. Let's look at that. First, how would you describe your own work style?

Nadia: I need to plan ahead and know what I'm doing and when. I need to know as much as possible about a project. I'm thorough and I'm painstaking and I want it to be as perfect as possible. And I get anxious if I put it off. **(Pauses to think and coach gives her time)** If I'm honest, I can be a bit of a control freak.

Manager: And his?

Nadia: He's laid back – a last-minute guy. Just plunge in and do it, that's him. He's clever and he has ideas but doesn't think them through. He's really good at presentations and just winging it.

Manager: On the face of it, that could be a good combination.

Nadia: Yeah. Oh yeah. I do all the hard work and he looks at it the night before and gets up and does his great presentation. Then he gets all the credit. I can have ideas, too. I can do presentations.

Manager: Is that what's making you angry? **(Coach sees he's touched a nerve, and acknowledges it, asking a closed question)**

Nadia: Yes. One of the things.

Manager: I can see that. So, going back a bit. Would you say that your work styles don't mix well? **(Brings the discussion back on track with a closed question, clarifying the main reasons behind the problem)**

Nadia: Yes.

Manager: OK. Let's brainstorm a few options to solve the problem. I'll write as you think. Afterwards, we can weigh up the pros and cons of each. Thinking about a solution, what could you do? **(Options to solve it and pros and cons of each)**

Nadia: I could ask to be taken off the project.

Manager: Quit the project. **(Restates to summarize and show he understands)** That's one option.

Nadia: I could ask to do the project all myself.

Manager: Do it all. **(Restates)** Two.

Nadia: I could leave it as it is and let it happen like I've just said – I do the legwork, he does the window dressing.

Manager: Leave it to sort itself out. Three. Any more?

Nadia: I could talk to him and we could sort it out between us – if he can make the time, that is!

Manager: Discuss it. Four. More?

Nadia: No.

Manager: Right. Let's go back and look at them. First, quit the project. What are the pros?

Nadia: I wouldn't have to work with Rob. No hassle. I'd have time for my regular work.

Manager: Cons?

Nadia: It's a good opportunity and I want to do it. He wouldn't want to do it by himself. I'd lose face. I'd hate that!

Manager: OK. Second, do it all yourself. Pros and cons?

Nadia: I'd keep control. I'd get the credit. But I don't have the time. Rob wouldn't go for it. And... **(Pauses. Coach lets her think)** And I wouldn't learn anything from it.

Manager: OK. Third, leave it to sort itself out. Pros.

Nadia: None. That one's not going to happen.

Manager: Cons?

Nadia: Too many. Can we get rid of that option?

Manager: OK. Fourth option, discuss it. Pros?

Nadia: We could move forward. I could move forward. I would feel better. The job would get done.

Manager: Cons?

Nadia: He won't make the time.

Manager: OK. I've written them all down here. Shall we go through them again?

Nadia: No. I know what I should do. **(Has selected the best option)** Talking the options through has made me see I've got to talk to him.

Manager: OK. What would you say?

Nadia: I'd have to tell him how frustrated I am and not just say we need a planning meeting.

Manager: Good luck. Tell me how it goes, and if you want me to have a word with him, or with both of you, I can do.

Nadia: (Horrified.) Oh no! I couldn't let him know I've come whining to you! Thanks, though. I'm glad I did. It's helped a lot.

Learning Point

Once the options have been brought out, you can usually move through the pros and cons assessment pretty quickly.

Sometimes the answer will be obvious, without a detailed analysis.

Make sure to push the coachee for more options – see the COACH model in Chapter 1 for more examples.

Where next?

Bright Idea!

Download the DROPS work-sheet from www.Coaching Toolbook.com

Once the coachee has been guided through the DROPS sequence and selected the best solution, they may need further coaching, as James did in our first example. Use the COACH tool (Chapter 1) to help them with the next stage. You will also want to find out what happens next and to review the solution using the GOLD model (Chapter 2). The solution may have resulted in an objective, in which case you may need to help them tighten it up using the STORM goal-setting tool and to start putting together an action plan (Chapter 3).

History of the tool

One of the greatest military leaders in history, Napoleon Bonaparte, 'The Little Corporal', was born in Corsica in 1769. This tool is based on Napoleon's Completed Staff Work idea. Napoleon wanted to stop his generals bringing so many problems to him, so he asked them to go through a series of questions to see if they could solve it for themselves. It reportedly stopped 80 per cent of all demands on his time.

Related tools

1. COACH tool – see Chapter 1, page 1.
2. OPERA tool – see Chapter 6, page 79.
3. SWOT tool – see Chapter 7, page 99.

Further reading

1. Jones, Morgan D. (1998) *The Thinker's Toolkit: 14 Powerful Techniques for Problem Solving.* Three Rivers Press, CA (Paperback: 384 pages; ISBN: 0812928083).
2. Greene, Jane and Grant, Anthony M. (2003) *Solution-focused Coaching: Managing People in a Complex World.* Momentum (Paperback: 192 pages; ISBN: 184304028X).

Learning points summary

- This tool provides you with a logical sequence for solving a problem with your coachee, unravelling the issues, weighing them up and arriving at a solution.

- It can also be used by team members individually, so that they can sort out their own problems – which means that you don't have to!

- It is not always easy to get the facts straight in one go, particularly if coachees have been sitting on things for a while. You may need to question and prompt to get to the bottom of it.

- Often, thinking a problem through in the DROPS sequence will help the coachee reach a solution without completing all the stages. For example, having the coachee describe the problem fully, and listing any reasons, may reveal an obvious solution without the need to list and analyse a number of options.

- Another way it can work is that the coachee finds a solution in a combination of the options they have generated.

Take Action!

Use the model on yourself if you have a problem.

Write it all down and see how it can work for you.

Visit **www.CoachingToolbook.com** for a downloadable version of the DROPS tool.

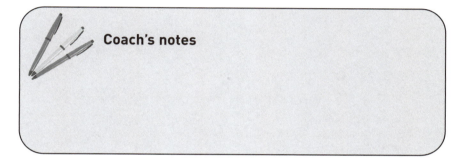

Coach's notes

Difficult decisions made easy

When there is a difficult decision, OPERA can make things simple

O Outcome desired

P Push forces for and against

E Evaluate each force

R Reduce or reinforce

A Action plan

Visit:
www.CoachingToolbook.com

You and your team members will often need to decide on a course of action when the situation is complicated and the waters are muddied. There will be a number of factors to be considered, and multiple stakeholders with widely different interests may be involved. The whole problem may seem overwhelming. When faced with such a predicament, how do you decide on the best way forward? What follows is an exceptionally powerful and flexible tool, which is applicable in a very wide variety of work and life situations.

When to use this tool

⇒ Any time you need to help someone think through a problematic situation.

⇒ When someone comes to you for help in making a difficult decision involving several factors.

⇒ When someone needs help with making a case for a particular project.

⇒ To help someone to drive change in a particular direction.

⇒ To help someone assess an individual's strengths and weaknesses, e.g. for a job hire.

⇒ To help someone assess the effectiveness of a team's combined capabilities and deficiencies.

How to use the tool

OPERA is a highly flexible coaching tool that can be used in many different ways. Central to this tool is the force field analysis model, which allows you to identify, assess, quantify and adjust the forces that drive and constrain a desired outcome.

The critical first step is to help coachees to identify their **desired outcome** – where they want to get to. The next step involves clearly identifying the opposing forces, **pushing for** and **against** (advantages and disadvantages of) the realization of that outcome. The next step is to **evaluate each of the forces** you have identified. Then you can look at ways of **reinforcing** the driving factors and **reducing** the restraining factors. After that, you can agree an **action plan**.

> If you have always done it that way, it is probably wrong.
>
> *Charles Kettering (1876–1958), inventor*

 ## Sample coaching conversation

Our first example shows how OPERA can work as a decision-making tool, where the coaching task was to help the coachee assess the forces for and against a particular decision.

The coachee wants help in deciding whether it would be more practical and efficient to work part of the week from home, rather than full time in the office. The coach helps clarify what might drive the desired outcome successfully forward, and what could restrain movement in this direction. Read through the following example to see how the coach moves the decision-making process smoothly forward:

Coachee: Coach, I am having trouble making a decision about the way I currently work.

Coach: What is it you want to do? **(Outcome desired)**

Coachee: I would like to work more efficiently. I currently spend a lot of time commuting to and from the office and too much time doing things that aren't part of my job. I have been thinking about working from home three days a week and I'd like you to help me look at that.

Coach: OK. Let's say the desired outcome is that you want to be more productive and efficient. You think that working from home might achieve that.

I'm going to draw a line down the centre of this blank sheet of paper. What I want you to do is to tell me all the factors you can think of that would push you to be more productive if you work from home. I will write them down as a list on the left side of the page. **(Factors pushing towards working from home)**

Coachee: First, I'd save two hours a day commuting time, so more time and less stress.

Coach: OK. What else?

Coachee: There would be fewer distractions – people asking me questions, asking for help with their projects or just to chat – and there are the meetings I get roped into that I really don't need to go to, so not so many interruptions. Also, if I need time to think, no one will wonder why I'm doing nothing! It's so hard to find thinking time at work with such a hectic pace all the time.

Coach: Fine. I've written those down. Now, what might stop you from working more efficiently from home? **(Factors pushing against working from home)**

Coachee: Well, I suppose I might lose the hard-working office atmosphere. It might be harder to motivate myself to get down to business. Also, I will still get calls from my co-workers and some of my occasional use files won't be to hand.

Coach: Anything else?

Coachee: I often use my commute to listen to audio books or pro-grammes. It's the only time I get actually to learn something. I don't have time to read books.

Coach: Got it. I've written down each of the forces at play on the page: forces pushing or driving you to work at home on the left and forces pushing against working at home on the right.

The coach has written down the forces for and against working from home as the coachee expresses each one. At this stage, the force field analysis looks like this:

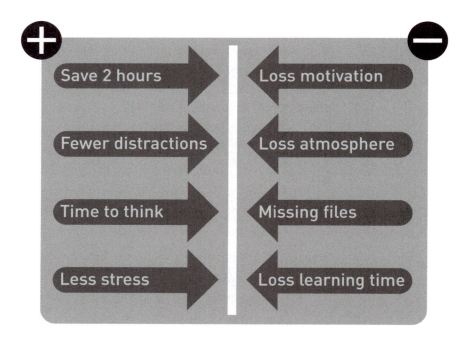

List of forces for and against: the **objective** is to be more efficient and productive through working at home.

The coach continues with the dialogue:

Coach: Now I'd like you to evaluate each of the factors we've written down in terms of their weight and importance. 'A' for the weightiest and most important, 'B' for not so important and 'C' for unimportant. I'll give you a few minutes to do this. **(Evaluate the forces)**

The coachee spends three or four minutes doing this. The resulting A-B-C weightings are shown on the diagram below:

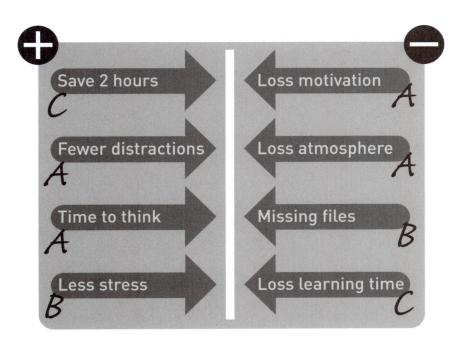

The dialogue continues.

Coachee: I'm not sure that has helped! I've got equal weighting on each side!

Coach: That's OK – if the decision was easy, you'd have made it by now! The next thing to do is to look at each of the factors in more depth. **(Reduce or reinforce)** I see you've given 'save two hours' a 'C' rating.

Coachee: Yes. In terms of efficiency, it wasn't that important. I'd save time for myself rather than for work. I do use it to learn – but not as often as I'd like, which is why I gave 'Loss of learning time' on the other side a 'C' rating. They balance each other out. Other factors are more important. It's still a 'C'.

Coach: So let's look at those. I see that 'fewer distractions' got an 'A' rating. Can you tell me more about that?

Coachee: I think that's the main one on this side. I need long periods of concentrated time to prepare and write up plans, reports and proposals. In our open plan office, it's a nightmare getting those things done, so I get behind or miss deadlines, which I hate.

Coach: What would happen if you weren't there?

Coachee: Most of the interruptions aren't important. I end up rolling up my sleeves and helping colleagues with their problems or sorting out issues because I've had more experience. It's a problem that came up in my last performance review with you! I'd be accessible by phone anyway, so. . .

Coach: What I hear you saying is that not being there might be an added advantage and it could help your team members to do things for themselves. **(Reinforcing a point)**

Coachee: Yes. I'll be in for two days a week, so I could spend more time on those days dealing with issues and touching base with team members. It would make me more proactive rather than dealing reactively with things as they come along.

Coach: Does that make that factor more important?

Coachee: Yes. I'd give it an 'A star'!

Coach: OK. What about 'time to think'? You gave that an 'A' rating.

Coachee: Yes. I'd leave that as an 'A'.

Coach: What about 'Less stress'?

Coachee: I'll leave that as a 'B' – it's more of a 'nice to' rather than a 'need to' for now.

Coach: Now let's look at the factors on the other side.

Coachee: Well. I gave loss of motivation an 'A', but I think I could demote that to a 'B'. I'm motivated by deadlines, anyway, so I don't think it's that important. **(Reduce the weight of a point)**

Coach: What about the others?

Coachee: Loss of atmosphere. Yes, I'd miss the buzz. Leave it an 'A'. The other two don't seem that important, now that I've talked this through with you. Files – I'll have to be organized about what I need beforehand, and get any others sent to me via email, if necessary. Learning time – I can do that in the bath! Both 'C'.

Coach: So, you've got an 'A star', an 'A' and a 'B' in favour of working from home, and an 'A', two 'Bs' and a 'C' against.

Learning Point

Power is the faculty or capacity to act, the strength and potency to accomplish something. It is the vital energy to make choices and decisions. It also includes the capacity to overcome deeply embedded habits and to cultivate higher, more effective ones.

Stephen R. Covey

Coachee: I think the decision is made! Working from home for some of the week seems a good move. I'm happy with it now I've talked it through.

Coach: Right. So what do you need to do now? I'll write as you talk. **(Action plan)**

Coachee: I'd need to work out how I'd organize my time. I'll make an appointment to talk to our head of department about it. After that, I'd need to tell the team.

Coach: OK. That's three actions. You're right to work out how you're going to organize things before talking to the department head. He'll need to know that you can make it work – we know what he's like! Let me know what happens!

Unpacking the example

This tool gives structure and purpose to any discussion about an important decision. The coach started by getting the coachee to identify the outcome – to work more efficiently.

Coachee: Coach, I am having trouble making a decision about the way I currently work.

Coach: What is it you want to do? **(Outcome desired)**

Coachee: I would like to work more efficiently. I currently spend a lot of time commuting to and from the office and too much time doing things that aren't part of my job. I have been thinking about working from home three days a week and I'd like you to help me look at that.

Learning Point

Don't focus all your energy on the mechanics of the tool! The sequence makes your discussion purposeful and productive, but remember it isn't as important as the coachee and the conversation.

Your aim is to help the coachee make the decision, not to make the model work!

The coachee has already been through an initial stage of the decision-making process on the road to reaching this outcome (the COACH model in Chapter 1 is an ideal tool), where he had generated options. He had chosen working from home as the most practical solution. The decision to be made was 'to work from home or not', so that was the focus of the discussion.

The coach explained the method and asked the coachee to list the factors **pushing him towards** working from home as a solution. He prompts him to think of more points by asking the invaluable 'What else?' question:

Coach: I'm going to draw a line down the centre of this blank sheet of paper. What I want you to do is to tell me all the factors you can think of that would push you to be more productive if you work from home. I will write them down as a list on the left side of the page. **(Factors pushing towards working from home)**

The coach writes them down on the left hand side of the page as the coachee speaks. Then he uses another open question, asking the coachee to think of what might stop him from working at home – the forces pushing against it. Again, the coach asks, 'Anything else?' which generates another point. As they talk, the coach writes the points down.

The next task was to evaluate the points on both sides. This coach chose a simple 'A-B-C' rating system. At this point – having identified the push factors for and against working from home – the coachee had an equal balance of As, Bs and Cs, which did not make his decision any easier. This is where the coach worked with him on each point to fine-tune them and to see if any of them, on either side, could be reduced or reinforced.

Note: You can use numbers instead of letters – A would be 3 points, B would be 2 points and C would be 1 point. You can then add up the points on each side of the central line and get a quantitative value for the forces pushing for and against.

During this stage, the coachee adjusted his initial ratings, with the result that he came to a sound decision based on the facts. The coach asks, 'So what do you need to do now to make it happen?' to help the coachee generate an action plan.

The model is solution focused. At any point during the conversation, the coachee could have been sidetracked into talking about the problems he was identifying, or may have been tempted to forget the outcome – to work more efficiently. Here, he was focused on his stated outcome and did not get bogged down in his problems. It is useful actually to write the desired outcome at the top of the OPERA analysis page.

Second coaching conversation

The second example conversation shows how OPERA can work as a preparation for persuasion or selling an idea, where the coachee needed first to identify the potential benefits for the boss, and reinforce them, and then to identify the potential objections and reduce them.

In the example, the same coachee comes back to the coach. He has raised the issue with their head of department, Riaz, and he has asked him to put together a business case for his proposal prior to a meeting to discuss it. The coachee wants the coach to help him persuade Riaz. The OPERA model can be used here, too:

Coachee: Hi. I've spoken to Riaz and he wants me to put my proposal in writing. I need to persuade him that working from home is a practical idea. I need your help!

Coach: Fine. Let's start by being clear about what you want to achieve, your **outcome**.

Coachee: I want to persuade him that working from home would be an advantage all round.

Coach: Can you be more specific about who will benefit? **(Question to help refine the desired outcome)**

Coachee: Yeah. That's me, and Riaz, also the department and the company.

Coach: We've already worked on the benefits for you, so that's easy. Would there be any difference between Riaz's interests, the department's interests and the company's interests? **(Clarifying question)**

Coachee: (Coach gives him time to think.) In theory, his interests are the same as those of the department and the company, so I need to focus on his interests.

Coach: OK. What I've written down is, 'To persuade Riaz that the department will benefit if I work from home.' Does that sound right? **(Closed question to confirm)**

Coachee: Yes. I'm stating the case for the department, but I need to reassure him, too.

Coach: Right. I think we need briefly to clarify what those interests are. If we list them first, we can analyse later. **(States a clear procedure)** What do you think they would be? You've mentioned efficiency earlier. **(Leading question to establish the kind of information the coachee needs to give)**

Coachee: Yes – efficiency is important to him. Then there's productivity, time management and meeting deadlines.

Coach: I've got that. Anything else?

Coachee: Yes, there's teamwork. That could be a problem.

Coach: Let's put that to one side for the moment. I'll make a note and we'll come back to it later. **(Acknowledges and notes the problem and moves on)** I suggest we look at the benefits first. **(Push factors for the idea)**

Coachee: Yes. I'd be more productive, more efficient and I'd meet deadlines.

Coach: Good. For now, talk to me as if I were Riaz. **(Informal role-play to keep the focus on Riaz's interests)** I'll write the points down as you talk. Tell me how I would benefit if you worked from home. **(Probing question to elicit more information)**

Coachee: I'd be able to concentrate on specific tasks without interruptions, so I wouldn't waste time getting my thoughts back together every time I stop and start. I'd have specific tasks to do at home, and separate office tasks, which would help my organization and time management. I'd meet deadlines because I'd be able to focus on one task at a time and work faster. Also, when I'm in the office, I'd be more focused on what I'm doing there.

Coach: OK. I've got that. Anything else? **(Useful open question)**

Coachee: I wouldn't waste my time in meetings.

Coach: Remember I'm Riaz. Would he see that as a benefit? **(Closed question nudges coachee back on track)**

Coachee: I don't think so – but it might be a concern for him.

Coach: We'll get on to that next. We've got the main benefits for me as Riaz. Let's look at the concerns he might have.

(Push factors against the idea) You mentioned teamwork earlier, which we'll look at later. What else? **(Standard open coaching question when eliciting more information or options)**

Coachee: Less contact with the team, yes. Availability. Liaising with other departments. Missing meetings. And you'd be worried about losing control.

Coach: Call that 'loss of contact with Riaz'. I've got those. OK. Now rate each one 'A', 'B' or 'C', like you did before. **(Evaluate the forces)**

The coachee's force field analysis now looks like this:

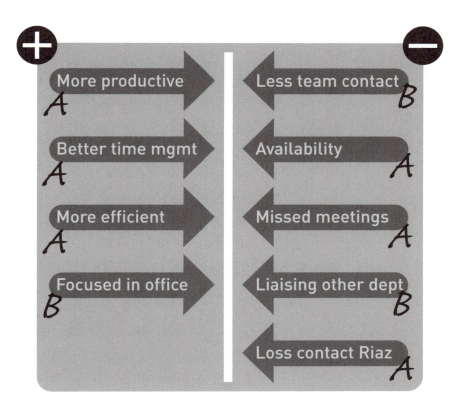

The dialogue continues:

Coach: Good. We've got three 'As' and a 'B' on the left and three 'As' and two 'Bs' on the right. Let's see how we can maximize the forces for the idea. **(Reinforce the forces)** Starting at the top, what can you do to strengthen each one?

Coachee: Productivity, time management and efficiency are strong anyway. I gave 'more focused when in the office' a 'B'. I think I could also say that I'd be more involved with the team when I am in the office. It would still be a 'B', though.

Coach: OK, let's move on to the right hand side. How can you minimize these concerns? **(Reduce the forces against)**

Coachee: I think 'less contact with the team' balances out 'more focused when in the office'. So, I could point out that even though I won't be there as much, I'd be more involved and less preoccupied when I am.

Coach: Great. Go on.

Coachee: Availability – I'd be contactable on the phone and by email. Availability to other team members – Riaz knows I get too involved in other people's projects, so that's not an issue for him. I think I could demote that point to a 'B'.

Coach: Got that. Missed meetings?

Coachee: The important meetings are arranged ahead of time, so I could plan to be there for those. Team meetings are on Mondays, so that could be an office day. I don't think I need to be at any others. I think that's a 'B', too.

Coach: We're making progress here. Liaising with other departments? That's a 'B' now.

Coachee: I do that by phone, normally, or in a planned meeting, so it's not an issue for me, really. I don't think it's much of an issue for him, either. Demote it to a 'C'. The next point is more important – loss of contact with Riaz – it's already an issue even when I'm in the office.

Coach: Is there anything you could do about it?

Coachee: (Pauses – coach gives him time to think) It may be easier to keep him informed, as I'd have to be more organized anyway.

Coach: Good. Go on. **(Prompts him to think more about it)**

Coachee: Actually, I could present that as a plus, couldn't I? So I can move that point to the left hand side – and it's still an 'A'.

Coach: Excellent! Now you've got four 'As' and a 'B' as forces for the idea, and three 'Bs' and a 'C' as forces against the idea.

Coachee: That's turned it around completely! I think I can put a really positive case forward now. I was feeling very gloomy about it. Thanks.

Coach: Good. I'll look over the finished document if you like. Can you get it to me on Monday morning and we'll go through it then? **(Establish time for completion of action step)**

Coachee: Yes please, I'd value that. I'll get it to you first thing Monday morning – my meeting with him is pencilled in for Tuesday afternoon.

Coach: OK. Write down your action points. 1) Confirm the meeting with Riaz. 2) Get the proposal written by Monday morning. 3) Review it with me on Monday. 4) Meet with Riaz on Tuesday. **(Generates an action plan)**

Learning Point

Give your coachee time to think of solutions. They know more than they think.

Only offer suggestions if they draw a blank.

Where next?

Once you have generated some action steps together, you can use the STAGES model (Chapter 4, page 45) to give useful feedback on the proposal. You can then use the GOLD model (Chapter 2, page 15) for follow up and review – for example, following the meeting with Riaz. This allows you to maximize learning by utilizing the way that adults normally develop – from experience. Set a date and time to talk together again after the meeting.

History of the tool

Kurt Lewin was a German social psychologist born in 1890, best known today for his force field analysis model. The author has taken this model and created the practical OPERA coaching sequence, which can be used in many different ways. Lewin devised the model originally to help managers identify the critical driving and restraining forces at work in advance of a decision and consider how best to remove or minimize the restraining forces and strengthen the driving forces. Lewin worked mostly in the USA, and his ideas still shape our understanding of group dynamics and play a part in organizational development theory nearly 100 years later.

Related tools

1. SWOT tool – see Chapter 7, page 99.
2. STORM goals – see Chapter 3, page 29.
3. DROPS problem-solving tool – see Chapter 5, page 61

Further reading

1. Lewin, Kurt (1999) *The Complete Social Scientist: A Kurt Lewin Reader.* American Psychological Association, Washington, DC (Paperback: 376 pages; ISBN: 1557985324).
2. Lewin, Kurt (1943) 'Defining the "Field at a Given Time"', *Psychological Review*, 50: 292–310. Republished in *Resolving Social Conflicts and Field Theory in Social Science.* American Psychological Association, Washington, DC (1997).

Learning points summary

- Use OPERA to help a coachee make a decision, assess a situation, identify forces pushing for and against a proposition, then to maximize the driving forces (push forces for) and minimize the restraining forces (push forces against) around the situation or proposition.
- The OPERA tool can be used creatively in any situation where the aim is to balance and adjust the forces working for and against a decision, an idea or a change.
- The tool incorporates Kurt Lewin's force field analysis model.
- Using the diagram, writing the factors down and rating them gives focus and structure to the coaching conversation, and allows the coachee to see the issue clearly.
- Use numbers instead of A-B-C ratings, to provide a quantitative measurement.
- The process of talking about each factor gives coachees time to consider and clarify.

- Reducing and reinforcing forces can allow coachees to change their perception of the situation.
- Use silence and give coachees time to think of solutions for themselves, when appropriate. Don't make suggestions of your own unless they have drawn a blank.
- Informal role-play can help coachees to focus on an angle or an agenda. Ask them to talk to you as if you were the person in question.
- Closed questions can be useful to check understanding, to keep the conversation on track, to change direction or to close a topic.
- Don't forget to make a hard copy action plan, otherwise it's just talking!
- Follow up and show interest, even if it's only a conversation in the corridor.

Take Action!

Write something now – your thoughts on OPERA based coaching. How else can you use the OPERA tool? Use the model on yourself if you have a difficult decision to make.

Visit **www.CoachingToolbook.com** for a download-able version of the OPERA tool.

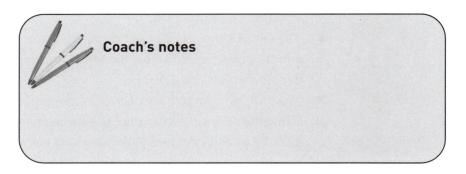

Coach's notes

Decision making now and in the future

Too close to see where you are now? Unclear of your position? Stand back and SWOT it!

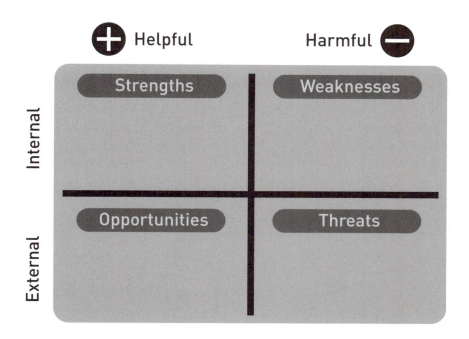

Visit:
www.CoachingToolbook.com

SWOT is a beautifully simple and flexible framework for analysing an organization, a team, a person's capabilities or an idea prior to setting a direction for strategy, decision making or creating a workable action plan.

When to use this tool

⇒   Any time a team member needs to take stock of a current situation with a view to planning for the future.

⇒   For analysing a team member's current capability and situation before or during a career development review.

⇒   When a team leader wants to assess the capabilities of and gaps in their team before recruiting another member.

⇒   When a team member wants to analyse the viability of an idea.

How to use the tool

This tool helps you and your coachee to assess a situation, an idea, a person or an organization's position regarding the future, and to analyse the available data logically, thus enabling you to understand, discuss, evaluate and make decisions.

First, you need to examine the team, person, idea or organization in terms of its intrinsic **strengths** and **weaknessess** – the internal factors in operation that contribute to the success of the idea or venture. Next, you analyse the possible operating factors in terms of the external and future **opportunities**, followed by the external **threats** that may block success.

This gives you a clear understanding of the strengths and weaknesses of the proposition – the internal environment – providing a picture of past and present experiences. The opportunities and threats highlight the external environment and future potential of the proposition. Once you have evaluated a SWOT grid, you can then generate a strategy or action plan, or make a decision based on the information it provides.

Beware: Make sure you are very clear of your focus – the purpose of the exercise. Keep checking the subject of your SWOT analysis. It's easy to stray away from it, particularly when you come to listing the opportunities.

> It is not the answer that enlightens, but the question.
>
> *Eugene Ionesco Decouvertes (1909–1994),*
> *French (Romanian-born) dramatist*

Sample coaching conversation

In the following conversation, Ali is not sure whether to apply for the post of team leader that has recently come up. It represents a promotion and he wants to analyse his own position to see whether it would be a good move (the focus of this SWOT analysis). Ali approaches one of the company's coaching managers, a friend of his, to get some advice:

Ali: I'd like you to help me decide whether to go for the team leader job. I'd like to try, but I'm not sure if I'm ready for it.

Coach: So you'd like to assess your position?

Ali: Yes. I only want to go for it if I have a good chance.

Coach: OK. I suggest we look at your own capabilities and experience first – your strengths and weaknesses for the role of team leader. Then we can look at the opportunities for the future and any threats that it presents, to see if this is a good move for you. I'll write as you talk.

Ali: Fine. **(This section has clearly established the focus of the SWOT analysis)**

Coach: Right. **What would your strengths be**, in relation to the job of team leader?

Ali: Well, I know about all the different jobs within the team, because I've done all of them! I'm good at seeing how they fit together and looking at what happens next.

Coach: Good. You know the team tasks, how the team works and see the bigger picture. What else?

Ali: I get on well with my team. We have a laugh and they often come to me for help if they need it, because I know what to do and I can explain it well.

Coach: You get on well with team members. I've also written 'good communication skills'. Any more strengths?

Ali: I want to get on in life, I like challenge and I want to make the team work as well as they can. I've got some ideas about that. As a team, we have a really good mix of skills and I can see ways of making it work better.

Coach: Sounds like you've been giving it some thought already. I'll write down 'enthusiasm' and 'forward thinking'. Any more?

Ali: I can't think of any.

Coach: OK. If you do, we can always go back and add to the list of strengths. **What about your weaker areas?**

Ali: I've been thinking about that. I don't have any management skills, as such, and I don't have any team leader experience. That could go against me.

Coach: I've written 'no management training' and 'lack of leadership experience'. Anything else?

Ali: Kind of – it's about getting too involved and doing too much for other team members. And I don't want to admit it out loud because it really does feel like a weakness.

Coach: We're only doing this for you, remember – you don't have to disclose anything and neither will I. It's also good that you can recognize your weaker areas. I could write 'lack of delegation skills'?

Ali: Yes, but that's not quite it. (Pauses to think.) It's something about being too friendly. Do you know what I mean?

Coach: Is it to do with changing your role in the team – from a buddy to a leader?

Ali: Yes. That's it. I don't want to lose my friends but I don't want them to take advantage of me. I don't know how I'd get them to do things or maintain discipline.

Coach: If it's any consolation, that's a perfectly reasonable concern – and it says something about your judgement that you recognize it. It isn't easy, but there are ways of making it easier. I've put down 'uncertainty about change of role'.

Learning Point

Life consists not in holding good cards but in playing those you hold well.
Josh Billings

At this point, Ali's SWOT grid looks like this:

Strengths	Weaknesses
Knowledge of the team	Lack of management training
Knowledge of the team's work	Lack of leadership experience
Knowledge of team roles	Lack of delegation skills
Sees the bigger picture	Uncertainty about change of role
Popular	
Forward looking	
Enthusiastic	
Good communicator	

Don't be tempted to qualify or evaluate these factors now – save it until you have completed all four SWOT sections.

The dialogue continues:

Coach: Now let's look at the **opportunities** this job represents for you.

Ali: OK. Obviously, it's a good career development step. I want to move into management and get on. Also, it would be a good first move. It feels quite safe. I've seen how Gabrielle, the previous team leader, did things – she's very organized – and I think she'd be able to give me support and advice – she'd be my line manager, as that's why she's leaving the job. But I've got my own ideas about how to improve the way we work and I want to learn. I know the team members' strengths and weaknesses. I'm familiar with the work and the way the organization works. The team knows and trusts me.

Coach: I'll just read back what I've got down from that – there seem to be a lot of opportunities there for you. I've got 'good career move', 'safe and familiar territory', 'support from the current team leader', 'understand the team members' strengths and weaknesses', 'familiar with the organization', 'team members know and trust me', 'can put ideas into practice', 'opportunity to learn'. Can you think of any more?

Ali: No. I think I've dried up! I have given it a lot of thought, so all of that was on the tip of my tongue. But I'm still uncertain about the job.

Coach: That leads us on to the next bit – **the threats**. What could stop it being a successful move?

Ali: Well, as I've said before, it could be hard to move to a team leader role when I've been a team member. That's the biggest challenge for me. I also wonder if it might be too familiar, too comfortable.

Coach: What about the competition? Do you know anyone else from inside the organization that might apply?

Ali: Yes. I think Gary could be in line. He's been in the team for ages, knows the ropes and he's deputized for Gabrielle at times. He's a bit 'old school', but he knows his stuff. People from other departments will probably apply, too, but I haven't heard anything.

Coach: What about competition from outside the organization? Would that be a threat?

Ali: Yes, definitely. I think management might be looking for a new person to sweep the cobwebs away and push the team harder.

Coach: I'll make a note of that. Anything else?

Ali: Only that one part of me thinks it might be better to be a team leader in a completely different team, but I'm not sure I'd be considered. I'm a bit young and inexperienced. That's really the same as one or two of the points we've got already.

Coach: We seem to have come back to the beginning again. For 'threats', I've got 'maintaining discipline', 'too comfortable and familiar', 'applicants from the team – Gary, older with more experience', 'applicants from other departments', 'applicants from outside the organization'. OK?

Ali: That sounds about right.

Coach: Fine. Now let's look at the whole SWOT.

Ali's completed SWOT grid looks like this:

Strengths	Weaknesses
Knowledge of the team Knowledge of the team's work Knowledge of team roles Sees the bigger picture Popular Forward looking Enthusiastic Good communicator	lack of management training lack of leadership experience lack of delegation skills uncertainty about change of role
Opportunities	**Threats**
Good career move Safe and familiar territory Support from the current team leader Understand team members' strengths and weaknesses Familiar with the organization Team members know and trust me Can put ideas into practice Opportunity to learn	Maintaining discipline could be difficult Too comfortable and familiar? Applicants from the team: Gary, older, with more experience Applicants from other departments? Applicants from outside the organization – management choice/new blood?

Learning Point

Success in the market place increasingly depends on learning, yet most people don't know how to learn.

Chris Argyris

Unpacking the example

The SWOT model is a simple and methodical way of identifying factors around a topic and helping a coachee to reflect within a logical framework. The analysis is the result of that process – a completed SWOT grid. You can see the similarity to the OPERA tool method, where the analysis generates a number of items that may then be acted upon.

The first step – and a very important one – is to identify clearly the subject of the SWOT. If you don't do that, you're likely to run into trouble later on in the process, particularly when you're looking at the opportunities. In this case, it is relatively clear – Ali wants to analyse his own position in relation to the job of team leader. The question that the SWOT is based around is therefore, 'Is this the right move for me?' as opposed to, 'Would I be a good candidate?' where the opportunities would be the opportunities for the employer and not for Ali himself. The distinction is subtle.

The coach begins the core SWOT series by asking about strengths. You will see that the coach phrases the question carefully, so that Ali is directed to think of his strengths in terms of the job:

Coach: Right. **What would your strengths be**, in relation to the job of team leader?

Ali responds and the coach summarizes and writes the points down. Then she asks, 'What else?' for the first time, which prompts more points. The coach asks the questions, 'What else?', 'Anything else?', 'Any more…?' many times during this session, to help Ali stretch his thinking further:

Coach: Good. You know the team tasks, how the team works and see the bigger picture. What else?

Bright Idea!

Download the SWOT work-sheet from www.CoachingToolbook.com

He summarizes the points as they arise, before moving on to Ali's weaker areas. Ali identifies his most obvious weaker areas straight away – lack of management skills and leadership experience. The coach has to work a little harder to help him untangle his thinking around becoming a team leader to his friends. He reassures Ali that the information he uncovers is confidential, and is sensitive to Ali's obvious feeling of vulnerability. He validates his concern about this area and encourages him to be honest by saying that it's good he recognizes his weaknesses. He then suggests a form of words, 'lack of delegation skills', as a question, to prompt further reflection.

Coach: We're only doing this for you, remember – you don't have to disclose anything and neither will I. It's also good that you can recognize your weaker areas. I could write 'lack of delegation skills'?

This is offered as a tentative suggestion and is not the same as putting words into his mouth. It is perfectly acceptable in this situation and it doesn't matter that it is 'wrong', as it helps clarify his thinking. He then summarizes by paraphrasing it as 'changing his role'. At the end, the coach summarizes his notes about Ali's strengths and weaknesses before moving on.

Ali has thought about the opportunities this move presents and the coach reminds him in his question that they are looking at the opportunities for him. He summarizes these and moves on to the threats. Again, he poses the question very specifically:

Coach: That leads us on to the next bit – **the threats**. What could stop it being a successful move?

The coach then helps him to think about the threats in terms of competition from other candidates, by asking specific questions about applicants from within and outside of the organization.

At the end of the process they have a clear SWOT analysis which can be used in a number of ways – to look at building on strengths and opportunities and minimizing the weaknesses and threats, or to help him think through an interview situation.

Second coaching conversation

In this example, the coach is helping Gabrielle, Ali's team leader, to do a SWOT for Ali as team leader from the organizational perspective. She has interviewed Ali, Gary and several applicants from outside of the organization, and is seriously considering Ali as her successor. Let's listen in on their conversation:

Gabrielle: As you know, we've interviewed a few people for my job, and I've been very impressed with Ali. My gut reaction is to go for him, but I want to think it through and check it out, if that's OK.

Coach: Fine. Let's start by looking at what you think Ali's **strengths** are as a prospective team leader. I'll make notes as you speak and check the points with you as we go along.

Gabrielle: Right. He has a good grasp of the jobs within the team, he's goal oriented and is able to think at team level rather than just meeting his own targets. I can trust him to get on with things and use his initiative. He'll go out of his way to help other people in the team. He's been great with new recruits, takes his time and explains things well. He's very positive and good to have around.

Coach: Anything else?

Gabrielle: Well, he's been with the team for a year now and knows what the organization expects of him.

Coach: So he's familiar with the way things work. **(Coach summarizes)**

Gabrielle: Yes – and that's important. We don't want someone who puts the cat among the pigeons and starts making changes for the sake of it. I'm not saying that there's no room for improvement, but the team works pretty well already.

Coach: So, you're saying that you want someone to carry on where you left off? **(Coach restates what Gabrielle has said to check that she's heard it correctly, and then gives Gabrielle time to think and respond)**

Gabrielle: (Pauses.) Hmm. What I'm saying is that while a few new ideas would be welcome, I don't want to undo all the good work that the whole team and I have put in, creating a unit that works so well.

Coach: So do you think Ali could continue building the team? **(Coach steers the conversation back to Ali, building on what Gabrielle has just said)**

Gabrielle: Yes. We've implemented a few of his ideas already. He's a keen contributor. He's a bit too keen at times, but...

Coach: OK. Can I just stop you there? Is this a good place to summarize his strengths before we get on to his weaker areas? Can you think of any other strengths he has as a potential leader?

Gabrielle: Yes, of course. There is one more thing. I think he has leadership potential. I'm stressing potential here, but I think he could be good, with guidance.

Coach: OK. What I've got written down as strengths are 'good grasp of the team's work', 'goal oriented', 'team-oriented thinker', 'trustworthy', 'uses initiative', 'helpful and sup-portive', good communicator', 'positive', 'good contributor', 'good ideas', 'keen', 'leadership potential'. Is that right?

Gabrielle: Yes.

Coach: Great. Now we'll look at the downsides – his **weaker** areas as a potential team leader. You started to say some-thing about his being a bit too keen at times when I stopped you...

Gabrielle: Yes. He's a funny mixture. He can be a bit too keen and enthusiastic at times, not thinking things through, but then he'll surprise me by losing confidence. I've had to give him a lot of support and reassurance at times.

Coach: OK. I've written 'too enthusiastic at times', 'doesn't think ideas through', 'lacks confidence and needs support'. Anything else?

Gabrielle: Yes. I'm not sure he has the authority for a leader yet. He wants to be everybody's friend, but he will sometimes let other team members take advantage of his good nature. The combination of lack of authority and wanting to be a friend could make him a weak leader. And I'm not sure how the other team members would react to this promotion. I don't know if they would take him seriously enough.

Coach: OK. Anything else?

Gabrielle: No. That's it. I feel I've made more of his weaknesses than they deserve – he could come into his own if he had the extra responsibility and authority that goes with it. **(She pauses, frowning. Coach gives her time to think)** He interviewed very well, I thought. (Pauses.) Oh, I don't know!

Coach: Remember, you don't have to make the decision right now. Let's look at the strengths and weaknesses before we move on.

Ali's SWOT grid, from the point of view of an employer, now looks like this:

Strengths	Weaknesses
Good grasp of the team's work	Too young, lacks experience
Goal oriented	Too enthusiastic
Team-oriented thinker	Doesn't always think ideas through
Trustworthy	Lacks confidence
Uses initiative	Needs support
Helpful and supportive	Lacks authority
Good communicator	Wants to be liked/a friend
Positive	Lets others take advantage of him
Good contributor	Others may not take him seriously
Good ideas	
Keen	
Leadership potential	

The dialogue continues:

Learning Point

Coach helps to direct Gabrielle's thoughts by choosing her words carefully, specifying the focus of the opportunities.

Coach: Now we can look at **the opportunities** from your own and the organization's point of view.

Gabrielle: First – this organization needs people like him. We'd be growing a bright employee for future management or leadership positions – we don't want to lose him or waste his potential. He's familiar with the organizational culture already and fits in well. He has good ideas and communicates well. He can think strategically and is financially clued up. I doubt if we'd be able to attract anyone as potentially as good as he is from the outside without offering a better package – so he represents value for money.

Coach: Quite a lot of opportunities, then! I'm having trouble keeping up! Any more?

Gabrielle: Probably – but I can't think of more at the moment. I feel very strongly that we shouldn't lose him and that he'll go if we don't give him something to stay for.

Coach: Yes – more to discuss and mull over, it seems. But before we get into the evaluation and decision making, let's look at **the threats** that his appointment as team leader might present to you, the team and the organization.

Gabrielle: You mean the possible threats to us if we appoint him?

Coach: Yes, that's right. You've started thinking about that already when we were discussing Ali's weaker areas. You mentioned his lack of confidence and experience earlier. What could that mean for the organization and the team?

Gabrielle: Yes. His lack of experience and confidence could mean that it could all go downhill. The team would have a weak leader and stop working effectively.

Coach: Go on.

Gabrielle: And we could lose the momentum. The team spirit would be sabotaged. Productivity would go down. People might leave. I don't like thinking about it!

Coach: Yes, but it's better to make yourself aware of the risks now than to wish you'd thought it through better at a later date. You can't make any decision risk-free, but you can weigh them up rationally.

Gabrielle: Yes. I've also just thought of the threats to us if we promote a good person too soon and it's a disaster – we could lose all that potential.

Coach: I think you're going too far into that scenario. Let's just concentrate on listing the threats, then we can look at the whole picture and possible scenarios later.

Learning Point

Coach gives Gabrielle a steer.

The SWOT is focused on 'Ali as team leader' so as to give a full picture of that position. At this point, it is not a debate, an evaluation or a discussion. It would be easy to muddy the issue by thinking of the threats in terms of for and against his appointment and losing the thread.

Gabrielle: Yes. You're right. What have I said so far?

Coach: OK. We've got 'the team could stop working effectively', 'productivity would go down', 'momentum and motivation could be lost', 'loss of team members', 'more pressure on line management' and finally 'possible waste of Ali's potential'.

Gabrielle: That sounds about right. There's also the loss of Ali as a great team member.

Coach: Good one. Any more?

Gabrielle: No.

Coach: Good. Now we can look at the whole picture.

Ali's completed SWOT analysis – his appointment as team leader from the point of view of the employer – looks like this:

Strengths	Weaknesses
Good grasp of the team's work Goal oriented Team-oriented thinker Trustworthy Uses initiative Helpful and supportive Good communicator Positive Good contributor Good ideas Keen Leadership potential	Too young, lacks experience Too enthusiastic Doesn't always think ideas through Lacks confidence Needs support Lacks authority Wants to be liked/a friend Lets others take advantage of him Others may not take him seriously

Opportunities	Threats
Growing a leader for the future Familiar with organization and culture Source of good new ideas Good communication Strategic input Financial ability Unable to attract anyone as good from the outside Value for money	The team could stop working effectively Productivity could go down Team motivation could be lost Possible loss of team members Pressure on line management Possible waste of Ali's potential Loss of Ali as a great team member

Where next?

Once you have generated a SWOT, you can use it in a variety of different ways: to evaluate options prior to decision making, to set strategy and to see how you can maximize strengths and opportunities and minimize the weaknesses and threats.

The primary result doing a SWOT analysis is typically the generation of a number of action items to achieve a certain objective.

History of the tool

The SWOT tool is a familiar, simple and effective tool, tried and tested in many situations since it was initially developed. It began its life in the 1960s as SOFT – Satisfactory, Opportunity, Fault and Threat – at the Stanford Research Institute as the 'planning issue analysis' step of a more complex and integrated corporate planning method. It then evolved as SWOT and was promoted in Britain by Urick and Orr in 1970 as a tool in and of itself. It has been used as an organizational analysis tool in board rooms across the world, and has been adapted freely and often to fit an enormous range of situations.

Related tools

1. COACH tool – see Chapter 1, page 1.
2. OPERA tool – see Chapter 6, page 79.
3. STAGES for performance reviews – see Chapter 8, page 121.
4. STORM tool – see Chapter 3, page 29.

Further reading

1. Porter, Michael E. (2004) *Competitive Strategy: Technique for Analyzing Industries and Competitors.* The Free Press (Paperback: 416 pages; ISBN: 0743260880).
2. Coyle, Geoff (2003) *Practical Strategy: Structured Tools and Techniques.* FT Prentice Hall (Paperback: 308 pages; ISBN: 0273682202.)

Learning points summary

- SWOT is a useful tool for analysing an organization, a team, a person's capabilities or an idea prior to setting a direction for strategy, making a decision or creating a workable action plan.
- Strengths and weaknessess are the current and internal factors involving past experience and the present position.
- Opportunities and threats are factors involving the future and the external environment that may contribute positively or negatively to success.
- Make sure you are very clear of the purpose of the exercise – keep checking the subject of your SWOT analysis.
  - Don't be tempted to qualify or evaluate the factors as you identify them – save it until you have completed all four SWOT sections.

Bright Idea!

Use the SWOT model on yourself now if you need to analyse your own situation, an idea or a proposal.

Visit **www.CoachingToolbook.com** for a downloadable version of the SWOT tool.

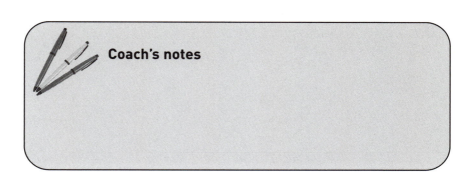

Coach's notes

Taking the pain out of performance appraisals

Reviewing performance can be daunting – break it down into six easy STAGES!

S Set the stage

T Topic – specifically

A Ask for opinion

G Give evaluation

E Establish action plan

S Set review date or plan

Visit:
www.CoachingToolbook.com

Most companies have a performance review process, which is often regarded by both management and employees as an unpleasant chore. It doesn't have to be, as long as it is seen as a useful two-way process. Used effectively, alongside frequent and timely ongoing feedback, it can be a highly productive forum for discussion and debate. The STAGES model for performance reviews will help you to structure these sessions to achieve exactly that.

When to use this tool

⇒ As a structure for a formal performance review.
⇒ Whenever you need to review a team member's performance.
⇒ When you need to review performance and progress after induction and a trial period.
⇒ For performance improvement reviews, prior to possible disciplinary action.

How to use the tool

The STAGES coaching tool for performance reviews will guide you through a logical sequence of steps, developed to involve both you and your team member fully in the process. Simple and flexible, it can easily complement a proprietary company review procedure and be robust enough to stand alone.

Note: You will see the strong similarity to the STAGES feedback tool (from which it is derived). The emphasis, however, is in setting the stage for the appraisal – clarifying the purpose and sequence that the process will take. Due to the formal nature of performance reviews, the emotional and physical setting (required in the first 'S' of the STAGES everyday feedback tool) has already been addressed.

First, you will need to **set the stage** – outline and explain what will happen during the session. The next five steps can then be used for each topic or competency area. The specific **topic** is clearly identified each time. Then you **ask for their opinion**, his or her assessment of their own performance in that area. You then **give your evaluation** of that performance. The next step is to **establish an action plan**, and finally, you need to **set a review date or a plan** for ongoing follow up.

> I am still learning...
>
> *Michelangelo (1475–1564), Italian sculptor, painter, architect and poet*

Sample coaching conversation

Read through the following example, which shows how the STAGES tool can be used at the beginning of a paper-based formal performance review. The manager is reviewing a new team leader's performance for the quarter:

Tom: Hello. Here we are again! I've done some preparation this time, too!

Manager: Good. We've got about an hour to discuss how you've been doing and agree an action plan. I need your help with this – it's a discussion – and I'd also like you to tell me what I can do to help you with your goals.

First, I'd like to get through the paperwork part. I suggest we tackle your overall performance first, and

Bright Idea!

Download the STAGES appraisal worksheet from www.CoachingToolbook.com

work through each competency area in turn. I'll outline the topic, after which you can give your own assessment of your performance on each element. After that, I'll evaluate it, we can discuss the two evaluations, and we'll agree an action plan and set dates for ongoing review. **(Coach sets the stage)**

Let's start with your overall performance. **(Outlines the specific topic)** How do you think you have performed since our last review? **(Asks for opinion)** Forget the rating scales for now. Just tell me in your own words.

Tom: Overall, I'm pleased. The team has consistently met all its productivity targets this quarter and, as team leader, I've played a part in that. I'm doing well on the team communication side – I run regular meetings and I think most of my team members feel able to contribute, although there is one notable exception. I expect we'll come to that later. I get things done and provide support as a leader. I'm getting better at pacing myself and spending time on planning. That's about it.

Manager: OK. Your comments aren't so different from mine. Overall, I'm proud of how you've got to grips with the new role. I think you've made great progress. You've always been a good communicator and I agree that you've developed that skill in a team setting. The team has got things done, without fuss and, as you say, that's got a lot to do with you.

I know the person that you're talking about when you say one of the team members doesn't contribute as much as you'd like. We may be able to find a way of tackling that later in the session. However, you missed out one element, on the second page. **(Gives evaluation)**

Tom: (Looks at review document for the first time. Turns over the page.) Oh, yes! Paperwork and management reporting. I get behind.

Manager: (Smiling.) I think the fact that you forgot to mention it says a lot! What happens with this?

Tom: I just can't seem to get the management reports in on time every week. I'll do it one week, then forget that I have to do it the following Thursday – and it's Friday before I remember. Then I get the sharp reminder from Head Office, which really gets to me. I resent it.

Manager: What I don't understand is how you're meticulous about getting in reports on your team members and you get your stock reports in, but you don't get management reports in. Tell me about that.

Tom: Well, if I don't get reports on team members in, they suffer. I can connect them with real people and I see the point of them. Stock reports are a pain, but if I don't do those, I don't get my stock replenished and it affects us. Management reports just disappear into Head Office.

Manager: OK. Two things. First, perhaps we can find a way to make these reports mean something to you. Second, we need to look at how I can help you to get them done. I'll write the second point down as an action point now. **(Establish an action plan)** I'll make a note to explore the first one later, when we review that competency area in detail. Agreed?

Tom: Agreed.

Manager: OK. Let's sort out a first review date for getting the management reports done. I suggest we do it regularly and often. What do you think? **(Set a review date)**

Tom: Yes. OK. Can we meet every two weeks? I can make time on Friday 29th. **(Plan ongoing review)**

Manager: Good, 10 am, Friday 29th, then, for the first review.

Tom: Now let's start on the competency areas – Leadership. **(Outlines the next specific topic and the STAGES cycle begins again)**

Unpacking the example

> **Learning Point**
>
> Everyone thinks of changing the world, but no one thinks of changing himself.
> **Leo Tolstoy**

Let's look at an analysis of the conversation in more depth. The manager in the example begins by creating a climate of cooperation from the start. Note how he uses cooperative words and language such as 'discuss...', 'I'd like you to help me...', 'I suggest...', 'we'll discuss...' and 'we'll agree...' rather than directive language such as 'I'll tell...', 'I'll review...', 'I'll start on...', 'You give me' and so on, to involve Tom in the process from the start.

He then sets the stage for the session, even though Tom has had reviews before and presumably knows what's involved. It gives the session a structure and underlines its formality and importance, although the tone of the session is friendly and informal:

Manager: Good. We've got about an hour to discuss how you've been doing and agree an action plan. I need your help with this – it's a discussion – and I'd also like you to tell me what I can do to help you with your own goals.

First, I'd like to get through the paperwork part. I suggest we tackle your overall performance first, and work through each competency area in turn. I'll outline the topic, after which you can give your own assessment of your performance on each element. After that, I'll evaluate it, we can discuss the two evaluations, and we'll agree an action plan and set dates for ongoing review. **(Coach sets the stage)**

He then states the first topic, which in this case was a general review of Tom's performance. Next, he asks Tom his opinion of his performance in his own words. Tom gives a rundown of how he has done.

The manager then gives his own evaluation, which is quite similar. Note that he tells Tom that he's proud of his performance and specifically mentions his grasp of the new role, his good communication skills and task-oriented approach:

Manager: OK. Your comments aren't so different from mine. Overall, I'm proud of how you've got to grips with the new role. I think you've made great progress. You've always been a good communicator and I agree that you've developed that skill in a team setting. The team has got things done, without fuss and, as you say, that's got a lot to do with you. . . . **(Gives evaluation)**

Clearly, Tom is good at what he does, but he appears to have a somewhat cavalier attitude to completing and sending in his weekly management reports. The manager coach flags up the fact that he has forgotten to mention this in his overall review. The conversation then veers off the overall evaluation, focusing instead on his attitude to the reports. The manager decides to strike while the iron is hot, identifying two possible actions – one of which he 'parks' for discussion later, and the other he pursues, so establishing an action plan. They agree and set a review date and plan for that action, which brings that part of the review to an end. Then the cycle begins again when the manager identifies the next topic.

Second coaching conversation

The second example conversation shows how the STAGES tool can be used in a formal performance improvement review. As it is formal and must comply with company policy, the manager pays attention to setting the stage at the outset:

Learning Point

Make sure the desired outcome is specific.

Manager: Tanya, you're here because over the last few months, your performance has not been satisfactory, and you have received a letter inviting you to attend this meeting. Pavel is here from HR as a witness, and he will take notes. You decided not to have a colleague with you. Is that right? **(Opening statement to help set the stage)**

Tanya: Yes. I didn't want anyone else here.

Manager: OK. Do you understand the performance improvement process?

Tanya: Yes. It's like a disciplinary. I could lose my job.

Manager: Tanya, don't worry. This is not part of a disciplinary process. This is your first performance improvement review. You will have two more over the next three to six months. If your performance has consistently improved over that time, we will go back to the normal performance review process and the documents will be kept on file for six months. If your performance does not consistently improve, formal disciplinary procedures will start. **(Set the stage)** Is all of that clear? **(Closed question to check understanding)**

Tanya: Yes.

Manager: I'm here to support and help you. **(Clarifies the coach's role)**

Tanya: Yeah.

Manager: OK. We're here to look at your timekeeping and absence record over the last six months. I've got your line manager's report here, and you've been late 21 times and off sick for three days without phoning in to let your manager know. **(Topic – specifics)** Is that right? **(Closed question to check understanding)**

Tanya: Yeah, I suppose so, if that's what it says.

Manager: According to your manager, this hasn't happened before. You were never late and off sick very occasionally. Can you tell me what has happened? **(Asks for opinion, using an open question)**

Tanya: My boyfriend moved up to Lincoln and I take the kids to see him at weekends. I just can't sort my life out.

Manager: Go on. **(Invites Tanya to offer more information)**

Tanya: I get so tired and I just don't seem to be able to get to work on time. (She starts to cry.) I don't think it's fair to punish me for being sick.

Manager: (Passing her a box of tissues.) Do you want a glass of water?

Tanya: No. I'll be OK. (Blows her nose.)

Manager: We're not punishing you. We genuinely want to help you get back on track. **(Moves the conversation on)** Is

Learning Point

If your coachee starts to cry, offer a tissue and a glass of water (thereby acknowledging it) and CARRY ON.

He or she will usually stop. If not, ask if they would like to have a ten minute break. If yes, take a break and restart in ten minutes.

there anything else you want to tell me? **(Open question)**

Tanya: No.

Manager: We have to be strict about timekeeping and absence without contact. It really isn't acceptable to be late so often or to go missing for days without letting us know. **(Give evaluation)** Your work suffers and so do your team mates – they have to cover for you. **(Describes the effects of her behaviour)**

Tanya: I know. They're getting sick of me.

Manager: Have you thought of other options, such as going part time for now? **(Gives her an option)**

Tanya: Yeah, my manager said that – and asked me if I wanted counselling. No I don't. I really like my job and I don't want to lose it. I'll try my best.

Manager: OK. I'm going to make a note of that on your improvement action plan. **(Establish an action plan)** Is that OK?

Tanya: OK.

Manager: And we can review that three weeks from today. **(Set a review date)** If you're late during that time and still having difficulties, we can look at other options. If you want to talk to your manager, or to me, in the meantime, give me a call and we can arrange a time to talk.

Tanya: Yes. Thanks. I will try. Definitely.

Where next?

One of the problems with action plans made during annual or six monthly performance reviews is that they may not be looked at until the next one is due. Don't let it happen. If you are conducting an ordinary performance review, you can follow up using the GOLD tool. This can be used informally to keep the momentum going until the next formal discussion – when you can use it again! If it is part of a formal procedure, like the example above, don't let it slip. Make a commitment to seek out the individual and ask how things are going (but beware – show a genuine interest and don't nag). Set a date and time to talk together again after the meeting. You may need to set goals using the STORM model from Chapter 3, and do some more coaching with the COACH tool in Chapter 1.

History of the tool

This tool has been developed by drawing on the author's own experience as a coach and leader to smooth the bumps in the road to a successful performance review. The model sets out a series of steps used and tested over the years, such as setting the stage at the beginning of the process to give it structure and weight.

Asking for the coachee's opinion of their own performance before you evaluate gives them the opportunity to assess themselves, provides some control plus a starting point to generate discussion and comparison. You can avoid using an overly directive approach, which often stifles debate.

Once again, this tool follows the basic coaching method: work out where you are and where you want to go, and develop a plan for how and by when you will get there.

Related tools

1. STAGES feedback – see Chapter 4, page 45.
2. COACH tool – see Chapter 1, page 1.
3. GOLD tool – see Chapter 2, page 15.

Further reading

1. Fletcher, Clive (2004) *Appraisal and Feedback: Making Performance Review Work*. Chartered Institute of Personnel and Development (Paperback: 190 pages; ISBN: 1843980290).
2. Bacal, Robert (2003) *The Manager's Guide to Performance Reviews*. Briefcase Books, McGraw-Hill Education (Paperback: 180 pages; ISBN: 0071421734).

Learning points summary

■ The STAGES model for performance review provides a template that can be used whenever you need to conduct a review, and is adapted from the STAGES feedback tool in Chapter 4.
■ It can be adapted for both formal or informal appraisals or reviews.

- Reviewing performance is most effective when it is a two-way process.
- Used effectively, alongside frequent and timely ongoing feedback, it can be a highly productive forum for discussion and debate.
- The STAGES model involves both you and your team member in the process of discussion and review.
- Use cooperative words and language rather than being directive.
- Setting the stage gives the session structure and underlines its importance.
- The STAGES cycle can be used again and again within the same discussion – it begins again with the next topic.
- Action plans made during annual or six monthly performance reviews may not be looked at until the next review is due. Don't let it happen!

Bright Idea!

Who could you use the STAGES performance review tool with?

Visit **www.CoachingToolbook.com** for a downloadable version of the STAGES performance appraisal tool.

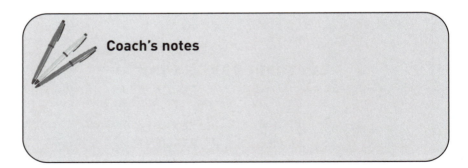

Coach's notes

Index

accountability 8, 12, 24

action plans 75, 82, 95–6, 98, 101, 118, 124, 126, 131, 134

action plans 8, 12, 42, 49–55

action points or action steps 12, 17–18, 27, 37, 57, 95–6, 117

activist learners 25

anger 71

Argyris, Chris 108

Aristotle 35

behaviour, changes in 21, 36, 48, 57

Berg, Insoo Kim 36

Billings, Josh 104

blame 65, 72

Bonaparte, Napoleon 63, 75

career development 37–41

chairing meetings 4–11

Churchill, Winston 2

clarifying questions xiv, 91

closed questions xiii, 56, 89, 72, 90–1, 98, 130

COACH tool 1–14, 26, 29, 40–1, 37, 48, 57, 74–5, 89, 132

communication skills 32–5

conversations, structuring of 3

cooperative words and lang-uage 127, 134

Covey, Stephen R. 87

decision-making processes 82, 89, 101, 118

delegation 22–3

de Shazer, Steve 36

DROPS tool 57, 61–77

Emerson, Ralph Waldo 18

emotional setting 64–7, 124

emotions, engagement of 21, 54

Epicetus 48

experience, learning from 12, 15–16, 25, 46, 96

external environment, opportunities and threats in 102

feedback 45–59, 96

follow-up action 17, 23

force field analysis 81–5, 93, 96

Forster, E.M. 24

goal-setting 20, 24, 29–35, 38, 75

GOLD tool 14, 15–27, 40, 42, 54, 75, 96, 132

GROW model 12

home working 82–96

Honey, Peter 25

hypothesizing questions xiv, 39

ideal outcomes 11

internal environment, strengths and weak-nesses in 102

Ionesco, Eugene 102

Kay Ash, Mary 32

Kettering, Charles 82

Kolb, David 25

leading questions 91
learning cycle 25
learning how to learn 108
learning styles 24–7
Lewin, Kurt 96
Lincoln, Abraham 38
listening xii, 68–9

Michelangelo 124
milestones in coaching 24
'miracle question' 11, 14, 36
motivation 14, 23, 24
Mumford, Alan 25

objective-setting 24, 31–2,
    42
objectives, personal 37
open questions xiii, 7, 22–3,
    27, 38, 54–5, 89–93, 131
OPERA tool 79–98, 108
opinions, asking for 49–51,
    53, 57, 124–5, 131–2
opportunities in a
    proposition 102–7,
    114–117
options:
    creation of 7, 18, 21, 23,
        64–6, 89, 131;
    selection of 8, 64–74
organizational analysis 96,
    117–118

outcomes:
    desired 11, 82, 89, 91,
        129;
    measurable and
        observable 6–7

paraphrasing xiv
'people problems' 71
performance reviews
    121–134
personal development plans
    37
power, nature of 87
pragmatist learners 25
presentations, delivery of
    18–20, 53–5
prioritization of issues 14
probing questions xiii, 18,
    22, 92
problem description 65, 69,
    71, 76
problem-solving 63, 76
progress measurement
    32–6
promotion opportunities
    102–113

questions, asking of xii–xiv,
    8, 76; see also closed
    questions; open
    questions

reciprocal behaviour 51
reflecting what has been
    said or felt xiv–xv
reflective learners 25, 57
resources needed 32–4, 38,
    42
results sought, definition of
    32; see also outcomes
review dates 50, 56, 124,
    127, 131
role-play 92, 98

setting for coaching,
    physical and *emotional*
    49, 44, 57, 124
silence, use of 11, 56
SMART model 41
solution-focused coaching
    11, 36, 65, 70, 90, 95,
    96
spoon-feeding 24
stage-setting 125–7, 134
STAGES tool:
    for giving feedback
        45–59, 124, 133;
    for performance
        appraisal 121–134
Stanford Research Institute
    117
STORM tool 29–43, 75, 132
strategy-setting 117–118

strengths of a proposition
        102–119
summarizing xv, 23, 56, 73
SWOT tool 99–117

telephone technique 49–51
theorist learners 25
threats in a proposition
        102, 106–110, 114–117

time for completion of
        tasks 32–7
Tolstoy, Leo 127
trust, climate of xii

Urick and Orr 117

visualization 35

weaknesses in a proposition
        102–7, 112–117
weighting of opposing
        factors 85–6
Whitmore, Sir John 12